The Hiker's & Backpacker's Handbook

W. K. MERRILL

Foreword by Fred J. Overly

WINCHESTER PRESS

To Leslie I. Ferrell, my lifelong friend, who has fought fires, ridden, hiked and backpacked the wilderness sky trails and helped me on search and rescue missions in my old Burnt Mill Ranger District, and to his good wife Hildred, who always had her home opened to those in need.

Library of Congress Catalog Card Number: 70-146063

ISBN 0-87691-031-2

Published by Winchester Press
460 Park Avenue, New York 10022

PRINTED IN THE UNITED STATES OF AMERICA

Foreword

A FEW DECADES AGO, this nation's population was largely rural. The people lived close to the land and by their own ingenuity and resourcefulness provided for their own being and their travel through the wilderness. A hundred years ago, the horse and wagon was the standard means of transportation.

Today, one jets across the nation in a trip of a few hours that once took months. The nation's population is largely urban, and we have become accustomed to existing in a highly organized and diversified society, with many of our needs supplied by specialists. This professional handbook has been written by a specialist who for many years exercised his ingenuity in the wilderness.

Ranger Merrill is well qualified in the art of hiking and wilderness travel. His long career as a U.S. Park Ranger in the National Parks of the West, and before that as a State Game Warden and a member of the United States Forest Service, has put him face to face with personal survival and the saving of other people's lives through search and rescue missions when they have strayed off the beaten paths.

While I was Superintendent of Olympic National Park in the State of Washington from 1951 to 1958, District Ranger Merrill was in charge of the vast Northwest District, with headquarters at beautiful Lake Crescent.

I know him and his wife, Margaret, well. These good people made a host of friends when they lived on the privately owned land around Lake Crescent. There, Bill was also the arm of the law, the United States having exclusive jurisdiction over the area. His law enforcement work, the protection of life and property, and the search and rescue missions he has organized are well remembered by his many friends at Lake Crescent, in Port Angeles, and on the North Olympic Peninsula.

Through this guidebook, Ranger Merrill imparts to the reader much of the wilderness hiking and backpack travel he has acquired by experience over many years. I commend it to you and to those who wish to hike the sky trails of our recreation areas.

FRED J. OVERLY
Regional Director
Pacific Northwest Region
Bureau of Outdoor Recreation
U. S. Department of the Interior

Preface

THIS little handbook will tell you how you can get away from your urban cares: away from sitting helplessly in snarled automobile traffic, from pounding the pavement in the canyons of the concrete jungles, and from rushing and pushing your way through city crowds; away from blaring television and radio, and the screaming of emergency vehicle sirens; away from tht smog laden air around the skyscrapers, and the polluted waters of the nearby river and streams choked with industrial waste and garbage; away from multi-colored signs and billboards and flashing neon lights; and away from the litterstrewn about by the careless. If life in the modern megalopolis makes you yearn to get away from city stresses for a while — far away — try hiking or backpacking into one of the nation's wilderness areas for a change of pace.

Often the difference between a full life and a cramped existence is measured in terms of our opportunities to test our physical strength against the elements of the wilderness. Many people have the hiking and backpack camping urge without the necessary know-how. Even the experienced outdoorsman, softened by his urban mode of living and office routine, may need a refresher course — a reorientation in the ways of the wilderness.

After 36 years in the Ranger Service, I have found that many of us need professional guidance on the out-of-doors so that we may enjoy hiking and backpack camping in safety. In this book, I will attempt to lead you over the right paths — telling you how to go light, but right!

To the old timers who have worn "the hiking boots of experience," I hope that the walking and knapsacking lore contained here will be tolerantly received.

The contents of this book have been reviewed by the U.S. Forest Service, the U.S. National Park Service, the U.S. Bureau of Outdoor Recreation, and the California State Parks and Recreation Department.

W. K. M.

Contents

An Introduction to Hiking and Backpacking

What Backpacking Means

GENERALLY, IT MEANS carrying your home away from home on your back in a knapsack — away from the improved roadside public campgrounds. It means hiking along through the woods on a mountain trail or in an alpine meadow or along a mountain stream or along the shore of a glacial lake into wilderness country where you can camp at will when night overtakes you. Backpacking is best described as advanced camping and should be undertaken only by those who are in good health and have hiked mountain or forest trails. It requires physical stamina and a genuine liking and love for the isolation of remote back-of-beyond country.

You Can Do It!

If you are tired of bumper-to-bumper highway traffic, of inhaling exhaust fumes, of "No Vacancy" signs in private and public automobile campgrounds, and if you are longing for a spot away from the urban type camping crowd, backpacking is for you. Head for the mountains! Leave your car at road's end and head up the trail for wild country where you can hike, take pictures, hunt, and fish without being trampled on. You will see much more when you travel along on shanks mare at 1½ to 2 miles per hour than you ever will zooming along at 65 to 75 miles per hour. If you are not an experienced hiker but the idea of backpacking has begun to interest you, there are so many places where you can ease into backpacking gradually, without investing in all the specialized equipment of the experienced and confirmed knapsacker.

Why the Knapsacker is a Different Breed of Camper

The experienced knapsacker is a different species of outdoor camper, and those who are not experienced, don't take long to become good woodsmen and mountaineers. Generally the knapsacker belongs to a hiking or mountain climbing club, or again, he may like taking off along the sky trails on his own. He enjoys getting away from the "fixed" camp and off the beaten paths where he can roam at will through the wild terrain of the primitive and wilderness areas of our national parks and forests.

Backpacking offers freedom found in no other type of wilderness travel. Unless he walks and leads a pack animal, the backpacker has no worry about tying up a burro or other pack stock when he pauses to fish in an alpine lake or mountain stream, take a snapshot of wildlife or brew a cup of tea. And there is no wondering if his horse or burro can pick his way over the rocks or across a snow field. There's no need to search for pasture when it is time to make camp, nor does he have to carry "catch" oats to supplement natural forage. (Hiking with pack animals has its advantages though, and they are discussed in Chapter 9.)

How to Enjoy a New Type of Camping

A thrilling new experience awaits the family who wants to get away from the permanent campfire grates and heavy rustic tables of the roadside camps where most people seem to camp. They want to get away from the noise of blaring radios and portable TV sets and late-arriving campers (supposed to be quiet after 10 P.M.) — away from the smell and dust of cars passing back and forth through the camp — away from fellow campers who let their young Davy Crocketts and Daniel Boones, with family pet barking at their heels, run screaming through your campsite playing Cowboys and Indians while old Rover stops to irrigate your tent, car wheels, or table legs, or leaves his calling card so that you accidentally track it into your canvas home.

The Cost

Backpack camping is one of the least expensive ways for vacationing. Food will not cost you any more than when you are living at home. In fact, it will not cost as much. The only extra expense will be that of transportation to wherever you plan to hike—the beach, woods, or high mountains. You will spend that much traveling to any vacation spot.

You Can Rent What You Will Need

You can go backpacking even if you are a city cliff dweller, living in a hotel or an apartment and lacking anything in the way of camping gear or even an automobile. Many sporting goods stores and outfitters rent outdoor equipment. In fact, if you are just starting out in the backpacking game, it is better to rent and see if this type of vacation is for you. You can rent an automobile, depending on the size, model, year and make for as little as $8 to $10 a day and from 8 to 10 cents per mile. All you need is a valid drivers license. Or perhaps you can go with a friend who owns an automobile or pickup camper and share expenses with him. And don't forget, you can head with your pack to many scenic areas by using public transportation!

Age Is No Barrier

Wilderness backpacking is not limited to athletes or supermen. While on patrol in California's High Sierras in Yosemite and Kings Canyon National Parks and again in Olympic National Park, I have seen babies carried by the father in a "Hike-a-Poose" knapsack or peeping out of a kyack on a horse or mule and from the pannier on a burro. These babes were not much over a year old.

Once on a Ranger's holiday, packing along the John Muir Trail, I talked to two senior citizens on Foresters Pass (13,200 feet elevation). One gentleman was 75 and the other 82 years young. Both were carrying packs of about 25 pounds. Personally, I would say this is pushing the hiking sport a little too far (I have had to pack out

Age is no barrier to outdoor adventure.

more than one hiker and hunter over the years from remote wilderness areas due to a sudden heart condition from overexertion — men many years younger). But the fact remains that backpacking has an appeal to all ages and can be tailored to the desires and needs of both young and old.

Rock, Ice, and Snow Climbing

This type of mountaineering is beyond the scope of this small handbook. Such climbing is a highly special-ized sport, and more than any other form of mountaineering, it requires experience and special equipment. No trail walker or knapsacker should attempt to rock climb unless he has gained the proper experience. By joining a mountain climbing club he can learn the proper climbing and safety technique from experienced club members or guides. *Remember,* it is always dangerous — actually foolhardy — to climb alone!

2

Hiking Away From It All...When, Where and How to Go!

Unlimited Opportunities

MANY EXPERIENCED KNAPSACKERS like the National Forest and Parks for a reason particularly important to them; they can camp most anywhere they please. They want more privacy than the park and forest automobile campgrounds can afford, and they prefer to put a pack on their backs and head into the high wild and primitive sections of these areas. There they revive the pioneer spirit of their forefathers by fending for themselves, whether traveling a little-used path a short distance from a main highway, or plunging into a vast wilderness area.

Hikers Like to Explore

Hikers explore old trails and abandoned tote roads and tramp their way across wooded and mountain terrain, making camp when day ends. Backpackers and hikers leading burros or other pack stock across mountain trails sleep beneath the stars, and return to their city home refreshed from the experience. Fishermen hike to remote alpine streams and high country lakes, and hunters take to the wooded hills and mountains in search of next winter's venison and bear steaks. They go in organized groups, in pairs, and alone. Families too, enjoy the away-from-it-all experience of primitive treks and deep woods' camping.

WHEN TO GO

Time your trip according to climatic conditions. For example, in the southwestern mountains, conditions are generally favorable for travel from June 15 to October 1, but in the northern Rockies the best time for a wilderness jaunt is between July 15 and September 15. Parts of the Appalachian Trail are open all year. If you go into the high country too early, snow may interfere with travel and you are more apt to get into difficulties or even into a survival situation. Streams tend to be high and difficult to ford, trout fishing may be poor, and meadows and trails tend to be soft, muddy and slippery in spots and subject to damage when walking or leading pack stock. August and September often provide the best weather for wilderness hiking, with little bother from mosquitoes and other insect pests. The desert wilderness of the Southwest shows its spectacular "bloom" in late winter and early spring and you are less apt to get into trouble than in hot weather.

But check closing dates of National Parks before you plan.

Winter touring, on snowshoes or cross-country skis is not discussed here, nor is winter camping, since these topics would need a full book of their own for thorough coverage. However, several excellent books are available covering the winter outdoor picture, and these are listed in the Bibliography.

WHERE TO GO

The National Forests — Forest Service Trails

For back country hikers and backpack campers, the U. S. Forest Service planned trail system offers approximately 165,000 miles of trails, of which 112,000 miles are standardized. However, in the 154 National Forests, substantial areas will always remain roadless. More than 14½ million-acres (over 22,656 square miles) of the Forests have been designated as primitive or wilderness areas. Wyoming, Montana, and California have the largest amount of wilderness acreage, but there are also sizable areas in Arizona, Colorado, Idaho, Minnesota, Nevada, New Hampshire, New Mexico, North Carolina, Oregon, Utah, and Washington. Local Chambers of Commerce are helpful sources of information about backpacking trips in these areas, and can provide names of guides and outfitters. Group trips are discussed later in this chapter.

The National Park Trail System

The National Park System contains almost 12,000 miles of scenic trails in the various Park, Monument, and Recreational Areas; of these 6,591 miles are well marked and maintained — a hiker's delight! For an

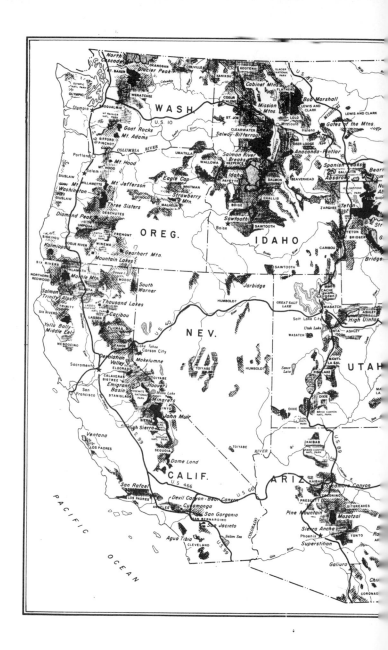

U. S. DEPARTMENT OF AGRICULTURE
FOREST SERVICE

NATIONAL FOREST
WILDERNESS

AND

PRIMITIVE AREAS

JANUARY 1, 1965

WILDERNESS
(UNITS OF THE NATIONAL
WILDERNESS PRESERVATION SYSTEM)

PRIMITIVE AREAS

NATIONAL FORESTS AND
PURCHASE UNITS

★ STATE CAPITALS
○ REGIONAL HEADQUARTERS

Scale - miles

0   50   100   150   200

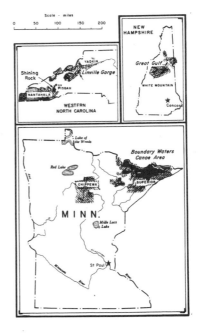

example, Glacier National Park in Montana, provides over 875 miles of wilderness trails. Besides these, there are hundreds of primitive side-trails for foot travel only for the rugged individual who likes to travel across country.

Ranger-Naturalists in various Parks conduct short one and two-hour tours that take the hiker into the midst of spectacular scenery. (Forest-Naturalists in some of the National Forests provide this same type of service.)

Something new for snow and ice enthusiasts has recently been initiated by Yosemite's Mountaineering School and Guide Service— overnight snow camping trips. Before campers leave on such a trip they take a special course covering everything from ski and snow-shoe use for level travel to building snow caves.

Hunting and Fishing

Why do some hikers enjoy pitching a camp far from civilization and rough it in the woods? Because they like to hunt. The National Forests, home for over one-third of the nation's big-game animals, are happy (unposted) hunting grounds. Other hikers like to go where the fishing is not crowded. National Forest fishing streams total 81,000 miles, and natural lakes and impounded waters cover nearly 3 million acres (over 4,687 square miles).

A complete listing of National Forests and National Parks, by state, is included in the Appendix of this book. Write them for detailed camping and trail information.

An uncrowded fishing spot.

The New National Scenic Trail System

Americans, especially young Americans have to see our natural surroundings as the first pioneers did to really appreciate this wonderful land of ours. They aren't going to learn about the country's great scenic outdoors from a car window.

Beautiful America is not a thing of the past, despite all you hear about crowding, pollution, and cutting of timber. A great bulwark of spacious beauty owned by the people of this nation still exists: the far-flung lands of the Federal government. One third of the land area of the United States — over 760 million acres (1,600,000 square miles) — is in the public domain and under the control of several government agencies in Washington. Much of this is untouched wilderness, and the largest part is still uninhabited.

Fortunately, in the not too far future hikers will be able to walk from Maine to California and from Florida to Washington State. Trails will crisscross the nation from one end to the other!

A new law recently passed by Congress and signed by the President gives us much needed opportunity to preserve and enjoy more widely many significant parts of our country's natural heritage. Many of these trails will hook up with Canada's Trail System.

Trails are relatively inexpensive to build. A splendid network of all kinds can be established at less cost than a few hundred miles of super highways. New trails are now being planned that will offer easy access to horses and bicycles as well as to long-distance hikers, backpackers, and those just out for a Sunday stroll. These hiking trails will provide the entire American and Canadian family with what could prove to be the most economical, most varied form of outdoor recreation imaginable.

Two of these famous trails already exist. The world-famous Appalachian National Scenic Trail is a beautiful hiking trail that extends over 2,000 miles from Maine to Georgia. It is marked by an identifying trail symbol

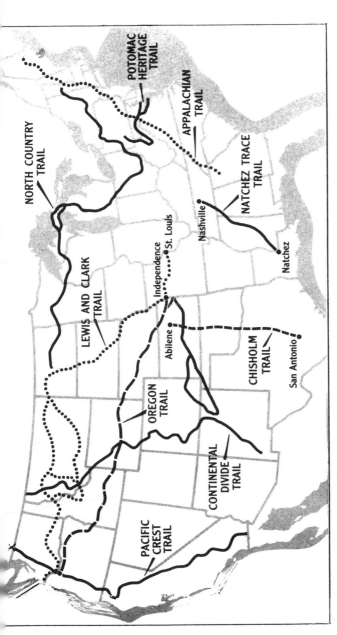

The new National Trail System. Two trails have been established as the first National Scenic Trails, the 2,000-mile-long Appalachian Trail and the 2,350-mile-long Pacific Crest Trail. In addition, 14 other possibilities for designation are being studied by the various agencies involved.

or marker and can be picked up from any of the many lateral trails connecting with it in several states. Here you can hike for as little or as long as you like.

In the West, the even longer and more rugged Pacific Crest National Scenic Trail reaches down from the Canadian border to the Mexican border for 2,313 miles with an additional 91 miles planned. In northern Washington, it connects with sections of the British Columbia trails. The Pacific Crest Trail serves both the hiker and horseback rider or pack animals. Motorized vehicles are not allowed — except to handle emergencies. Both the Forest Service and the National Park Service are in charge of trail sections that pass through their jurisdiction.

In addition to these trails and the hundreds of lateral trails connecting, 14 other possibilities for designation are now being studied. They are:

- Continental Divide Trail, a 3,100-mile trail extending from near the Mexican border in southwestern New Mexico northward generally along the Continental Divide to the Canadian border in Glacier National Park.

- Potomac Heritage Trail, an 825-mile trail extending generally from the mouth of the Potomac River to its sources in Pennsylvania and West Virginia, including the 170-mile Chesapeake and Ohio Canal towpath.

- Old Cattle Trails of the Southwest from the vicinity of San Antonio, Texas, approximately 800 miles through Oklahoma via Baxter Springs and Chetopa, Kansas, to Fort Scott, Kansas, including the Chisholm Trail, from the vicinity of San Antonio or Cuero, Texas, approximately

800 miles north through Oklahoma to Abilene, Kansas.

- Lewis and Clark Trail, from Wood River, Illinois, to the Pacific Ocean in Oregon, following both the outbound and inbound routes of the Lewis and Clark Expedition.

- Natchez Trace, from Nashville, Tennessee, approximately 600 miles to Natchez, Mississippi.

- North Country Trail, from the Appalachian Trail in Vermont, approximately 3,200 miles through the States of New York, Pennsylvania, Ohio, Michigan, Wisconsin, and Minnesota, to the Lewis and Clark Trail in North Dakota.

- Kittanning Trail from Shirleysburg in Huntingdon County to Kittanning, Armstrong County, Pennsylvania.

- Oregon Trail, from Independence, Missouri, approximately 800 miles to Santa Fe, New Mexico.

- Long Trail, extending 255 miles from the Massachusetts border northward through Vermont to the Canadian border.

- Mormon Trail, extending from Nauvoo, Illinois, to Salt Lake City, Utah, through the States of Iowa, Nebraska, and Wyoming.

- Gold Rush Trails in Alaska.

- Morman Battalion Trail, extending 2,000 miles from Mount Pisgah, Iowa, through Kansas, Colorado, New Mexico, and Arizona to Los Angeles, California.

- El Camino Real from St. Augustine to San Mateo, Florida, approximately 20 miles along the southern boundary of the St. Johns River from Fort Caroline National Memorial to the St. Augustine National Park Monument.

The Bureau of Land Management

Who says that there isn't any place to hike or go backpack camping anymore? Anyone making such a statement or even thinking it, has just not researched the subject! Besides the thousands of square miles in our national forests and national parks, there are the vast Bureau of Land Management Lands.

From the deserts of the Southwest to the tundra and wilderness of Alaska stretch over 718,750 square miles of public lands with thousands of miles of pathways and trails. Here the outdoorsman can find room to roam the wide open spaces and can hike and camp his fill. Here he can get away from it all. This is the public domain, still in Federal ownership — lands which haven't been set aside for national forests, parks, of other special uses. Here he can find variety, from deserts to forests, sagebrush canyons to snowcapped mountains with excellent hiking, backpacking, hunting and fishing in many sections of this vast vacation land. These lands are under the U. S. Bureau of Public Land Management, an agency of the Department of the Interior. A list of B.L.M. recreational areas by State appears in the Appendix. For more details, write to the Division of Information, United States Bureau of Land Management, Washington, D. C. 20240.

Private Timber Lands Open

What about another 80,000 acres of private timber land containing 40,000 miles of streams and miles of cutover timberland where game abounds and hikers and campers can enjoy nature in the raw?

Regional Trails

Whether you want to hike in Wisconsin, North Carolina, Colorado, or Oregon, regional trails will make traveling easier for you. Look for the identifying trail marker on whatever route you're following. You'll find it will lead you to some sights you might have missed!

HOW TO GO

Group Trips

Following a trail into the wilderness can be an exciting experience but it needn't be a difficult one. Several organizations have set up guided trips into remote regions in various parts of the country.

The Wilderness Society, for instance, offers 45 expeditions this year, including 14 horseback trips, 16 walking trips, 9 backpacking expeditions, 3 waterway trips, 2 ski outings and an Alaska tundra trek. The number of jaunts will vary in number from year to year.

The trips are planned for inexperienced wilderness travelers as well as seasoned outdoor enthusiasts. Local outfitters provide most of the equipment and make complete arrangements from the time you arrive at the starting point until the trip is over. You do not have to be a member of the Society to take part.

For listing of available expeditions and fact sheets on the individual trips, write to The Wilderness Society, 5850 Jewell Avenue, Denver, Colorado 80222.

Other organizations that promote hiking and outdoor tours include The American Forestry Association, 919 17th Street, N. W., Washington, D. C. 20006. For information on hiking and biking jaunts, contact the local branch of the American Youth Hostels, or its national headquarters at 535 West End Avenue, New York, N. Y. 10024.

Hiking and Mountaineering Clubs

The Appalachian Mountain Club is the oldest mountaineering club in North America and was organized in Boston, Massachusetts in 1876. Its object is to bring together for cooperation all those interested in the mountains of the New England states and adjacent regions, combining all their energies to preserve the beauty of its mountains and forests. The club builds and marks trails, huts, and shelters, and it publishes accurate maps of the region. It is considered the representative in the eastern part of the country of the interests of all woods and mountain enthusiasts.

The Sierra Club is the second oldest mountaineering club in the United States, was organized by naturalist

John Muir, who became its first president in 1892. Among the purposes of the Sierra Club are: explore, to enjoy, and render accessible the vast mountain regions of the Pacific Coast; to publish authentic information concerning them; to enlist the support and cooperation of the people of the nation and the government in preserving the wilderness features of the woods and mountains of the vast Sierra Nevada Range.

There are many other mountaineering clubs in the United States, Canada, and Mexico. In addition to the names listed below, you will want to check State agencies for Recreation or Planning and Development as a source of information.

United States

Alaska. Mountaineering Club of Alaska, 700 5th Ave., Anchorage 99502.

Arizona. Kachina Mountain Club, 2217 Encanto Drive, N. W., Phoenix 85026.

California. Sierra Club, 1050 Mills Tower, San Francisco 94120. The Sierra Club has nationwide chapters, active hiking, camping, and mountaineering groups.

Colorado. Colorado Mountain Club, 1723 E. 16th Ave., Denver 80202. Has several groups.

District of Columbia. Potomac Appalachian Trail Club, 1718 N. Street, N.W., Washington, D.C. 20036. Lists many clubs in the East.

Hawaii. Hawaiian Trail and Mountain Club, P.O. Box 2238, Honolulu 96813.

Idaho. Alpine Club, P.O. Box 2885, Idaho Falls 83401.

Illinois. Chicago Mountaineering Club, 2901 S. Parkway, Chicago 60607.

Iowa. Iowa Mountaineers, P.O. Box 163, Iowa City 52240.

Maryland. Mountain Club of Maryland, 3220 Brightwood Ave., Baltimore 21233.

Massachusetts. Appalachian Mountain Club, 5 Joy St., Boston 02109. New England Trail Conference (many chapters) Box 241, Princeton. 01541.

Montana. Rocky Mountaineer Club, 2100 S. Ave., W., Missoula 59801.

New Mexico. New Mexico Mountain Club, P.O. Box 4151, Albuquerque 87101.

New York. Adirondack Mountain Club, Inc., Gabriels 12939. American Alpine Club, 113 E. 90th St., New York 10001.

Oregon. Mazamas, 909 N.W. 19th Ave., Portland 97208.

Utah. Wasatch Mountain Club, 425 S. 8th W., Salt Lake City 84101.

Washington. The Mountaineers, P.O. Box 122, Seattle 98101. Spokane Mountaineers, Inc., P.O. Box 1013, Spokane 99210.

An information publication on hiking in the West is the *Pacific Crest News Letter* — subscription $2 per year. Write to Warren L. Rogers, Editor and President of Camp Research Foundation, Pacific Crest Trail, P.O. Box 1907, Santa Anna, California 92702.

Canada.

Write to the Canadian Government Travel Bureau's main office in Ottawa, Ontario, Canada, or to their offices in the various Canadian province capitals.

*Breaking camp in the Sawtooth Primitive Area,
Sawtooth National Forest, Idaho.*

Mexico

Get this information from the Mexican Consul in one of the large cities of the United States where a consulate is located.

HOW TO WRITE FOR MAPS

If you're on your own, you depend greatly on maps, so be sure you have the right kind. You can secure a good state automobile road map at your nearest gasoline station. This type of map will be good enough to route you to a State Park, National Park, Recreation Area or National Forest that you wish to hike in. From there on you will need a more detailed contour map from the road end where you will begin your backpack hike at the trail entrance into the wilderness. Chapter 8 takes up maps and map reading in detail.

Sectional Maps of the United States

By writing to the Superintendent of Documents, U.S. Printing Bureau, Washington, D.C. 20402, you can obtain a free list of sectional maps. Maps east of the Mississippi River may be obtained from the U.S. Geological Survey Service, Department of the Interior, Washington, D.C. 20240; Maps west of the Mississippi River can be secured from the Geological Survey, Federal Center, Denver, Colorado 80200.

Recreation Maps

Recreation maps may be obtained free from both the U.S. Forest Service and the National Park Service. Generally, these maps are quite small of scale, and you will probably need one of their larger contour topographic maps with a larger scale. These can be purchased at most Parks for $1. Maps may also be purchased from the larger stationery stores that sell office supplies.

Canadian Maps

You can obtain these maps from the main office of the Canadian Government Travel Bureau, Ottawa, Ontario, Canada, and the various provincial capitals from the same Bureau, and from the Map Distribution Office, Department of Mines and Technical Surveys, Ottawa, Ontario, Canada.

Mexican Maps

For maps of the Mexican National Parks and Forests, write to Direction de Geograpiay Metroologia, Tecubaya, D.F., Mexico.

3

Basic Rules for Hiking and Backpacking

Discovering the Wilderness

BACKPACKERS DISCOVER WILDERNESS in many places and in many ways. Some hikers may just want a day's walk along some forested trail where they can take pictures and picnic along the way; others will plan a jaunt through Oregon's Three Sisters Wilderness lasting a week or more; a few may try a climb up into the clouds of Mt. Rainier. Hikers may explore the rugged vastness of the John Muir Wilderness Area along the crest of High Sierras or search for the Lost Dutchman Mine in the Superstition Wilderness of Arizona. Hundreds of thousands of hikers and backpackers along the eastern seacoast enjoy various sections of the Appalachian Trail.

Don't Be a Recreational Casualty

An outing in the mountains can, and should be a memorable experience. Yet hardly a year passes without people being seriously injured and sometimes killed on treks into the high backcountry. Search and rescue

Go prepared when you head into the trackless wilderness!

missions are frequent and expensive, but unnecessary if only the forest visitors will be careful and not take chances or become careless. The National Park and Forest Services do not maintain a rescue helicopter, but they can sometimes arrange for one in serious emergencies when evacuation is impossible by any other means. Helicopters when available are expensive — $130 to $150 or more per hour — and costs must be borne by the group or individual. Military helicopters are available for life-and-death emergencies; however, distance and their involvement in other missions may delay their arrival at the scene of the emergency for as much as eight hours or more.

Planning the Hike

From start to finish planning should be done at home by consulting outdoor trail books, forest or park topographic maps.

Get all of the information you can on the area where you plan to hike. Allow plenty of time for normal hiking. Two miles an hour is about average for mountain hiking when carrying a pack. Allow time for terrain problems, as well as time out to take pictures and for rest periods. If your schedule is too tight you won't be able to enjoy the magnificent scenery along the trail.

As in any trip for pleasure or work, it is well to be prepared; the wilderness makes special demands on its users, and special skills are needed for certain types of wilderness travel. Before you start your adventure prepare your body to withstand vigorous exercise by taking progressively longer hikes near home. Choose your companions carefully for their mental and physical strength — their endurance as well as yours will determine what trails you may take.

Backpacking is strenuous, but it offers great freedom in choosing routes and selecting campsites, as well as doing less damage to wilderness than riding horseback. The backpacker can limit his speed to his own convenience, traveling as many miles a day as he finds comfortable and stopping where he desires. Hike-in camping builds its own wealth in the form of treasured memories, and alpine camping is an unending adventure, taking one to new territories, new sights, new sounds, and adventure.

Pack Loads

Proper equipment, with maximum utility and minimum weight, is mandatory for a successful backpack trek for all ages. Don't make a pack horse out of yourself! Many groups of people coming into the mountains are so overequipped with heavy unnecessary gear that they experience only drudgery instead of a relaxing outing. Common items of excess gear are large camp or belt axes (one per group is enough), transistor radios, heavy air mattresses, canteens (no need to carry water in most mountain regions), iron fry pans and grills (although a small one-man nesting aluminum cook kit per person can be handy.)

Youngsters under 14 should keep their loads under 30 pounds for a six- or seven-day hike. Older teen-agers can carry 35 to 40 pounds, but the heavier the load the less enjoyable the trip. When traveling with a group of women or teen-agers, the leaders may end up by having to carry any excessive items or to distribute them among the rest of the group, making everyone unhappy with the individual who toted along more than he could manage along the trail.

Clothing and Footwear

Proper clothing and footwear are essential to the well-being of the hiker in addition to making the hike enjoyable. These are discussed fully in Chapters 5 and 7.

Carry Everything with You

Make a check list before taking off to make sure that nothing has been left behind (See Chapter 4). Check each item off as you place it in your packsack. Examine with a critical eye for any unnecessary items and accessories that will help keep your pack weight to approximately 35 pounds which is close to the maximum for comfortable hiking. For the women in the party, the weight should not be over 25 pounds.

Energy Boosters

For a quick energy booster along the way add a small bag of chopped nuts, hard chocolate, and raisins to munch along the trail between meals. Make it a point not to eat all the "goodies" the first day. Gum will help slake thirst and boost morale. You should have at least one hot meal during the day, preferably early in the evening, consisting of energy-building food.

Caution on the Trail

Remember, the trail is just a narrow pathway through the wilderness, one that nature may redeem at will. The flower-draped trail of summer may in winter be covered with 10 to 20 feet of snow, in fall be hidden by pine needles and leaves, or in spring be buried by rock and mud slides. Look carefully so that you do not get off the beaten path and go astray! Dense brush and high grass will obscure unimproved trails. At times game will have their own trails — don't be misled into thinking that these are the main trail.

Trail Courtesy

Hiking requires certain courtesises. Step aside for descending hikers. Pack and saddle stock have the right of way. Step to one side of the trail where the animals can see you and remain quietly while they pass, otherwise they may "spook," disorganizing the whole pack string and possibly causing a serious accident.

Safe Hiking Judgment

Good judgment is learned from experience. If the weather turns threating, plan to go another time. Snow or rain may cause many adverse trail conditions. Windstorms can cause trees to fall along and across trails. DON'T become a storm casualty!

Use caution near slides and avalanche chutes. If your trail crosses a snowfield, look down — see where you are stepping. The wrong step or a slip may be your last!

Shaded snowfields are usually hard ice, and those easy-to-walk-on snowfields may have large cavities beneath them which can break through.

Trail bridges in primitive regions are frequently washed out. Take time to search out the best and safest possible crossing, where ripples in the stream indicate the shallowest water. Remove your socks and wade across in your boots for maximum footing on slippery rocks and mossy stream bottoms. Loosen your knapsack waistband for easy release from your pack. Use a sturdy limb or pole as a depth probe as well as a third support against the swift current. Good judgment at this point may save you a wet crossing, and the loss of your pack and gear.

Protect Your Pack from Animals

The comfort of your camp will depend entirely upon your forethought, experience, ingenuity and woodsmanship If you leave your camp for any reason, hoist your pack high in a tree out on a limber limb. Make sure the limb is away from the trunk so that a bear cannot pull the rope close and chew it through. Bears, raccoons, skunks, and rodents can find food deep in your pack if it is left on the ground, and deer will gobble up your salt, sugar, and other goodies. Alpine insects at certain times of the year will find you personally choice bait if you forgot to bring an insect repellent.

Back-country Manners

A wilderness outing can offer many things, but to most people the solitude and scenery are most impor-

Signs that guide without words have been adopted for use on public lands. Pictured here are some of those that have been adopted by the U.S. Departments of Agriculture and the Interior.

Recreation Vehicle Trail   Hiking Trail   Prohibiting Slash

Trailer Sites*   Firearms   Snowmobiling

Campfires   Fishing   Launching Ramp

Dam   Trail Bike Trail   Kennel

Campground   Hunting

Smoking

Grocery Store

Bear Viewing Area

Automobiles

Men's Restroom

Drinking Water

Trucks

Restrooms

Information

Tunnel

Women's Restroom

Ranger Station

Lookout Tower

First Aid

Pedestrian Crossing

Lighthouse

Telephone

Pets on Leash

Falling Rocks

Environmental
Study Area

Post Office

tant. All large parties have a decided effect — often unfavorable — on the many individuals and family groups camping and traveling through the mountains. The degree to which a group affects these other users is pretty much up to each individual member.

After going to considerable expense and effort to get into the mountains to enjoy peace and quiet (which they have every right to expect) people naturally resent the intrusion of a raucous group of adults or youngsters. However, if you show consideration for others by camping well off the trail away from other groups, and by being reasonably quiet, you will leave a good impression of your unit and organization.

The basic philosophy of wilderness is one of preserving nature unimpaired for the enjoyment of future generations. Man-made items are an intrusion on the natural scene. Certain things, such as trails and signs, are necessary for the protection of the area; but these are held to a minimum. In fact beginning in 1971, lands of the Forest Service, National Park Service, Bureau of Land Management, and Fish and Wildlife Service will initiate a new system of wordless signs to combat "visual pollution." A total of 77 universally recognized symbols will replace regular written information signs.

For this reason, please do not cut standing green trees, or pad your bed with cut boughs or other green shrubbery; don't engage in construction projects such as bridges, dams, lean-to's and trails; forget about improving campsites with homemade benches, tables, rock-lined paths or walls around your bed sites. The number of warming and cooking fires should also be held to an absolute minimum. The Park and National Forests belong to all of us, so help keep them clean. Pack out all your unburnable trash and help keep your forest recreational areas free of cans, glass, plastic, tinfoil, candy and gum wrappers and other unsightly debris.

A latrine and garbage pit should be prepared out of camp sight and well away from any stream or water source. After each use, it should be covered with a layer of dirt and it should be completely filled in when no longer needed.

Trash-littered hunting camp abandoned by slobs!

Don't Take Short Cuts

Cutting switchbacks damages the trails and takes more energy than staying on the trail. Besides it is against forest regulations. Don't construct trail markers along your route — these confuse other parties using the trail and must be removed by rangers or trail crews. If you must leave a message, instruct the last member in line to pick it up.

Don't Hurry Your Return

When heading homeward, rushing, particularly down-hill, can cause you to overrun a switchback, causing more delays or even a bad fall. Start your return early. Plan to be at your car at the road head before dark.

Aborting the Trip

Turning back before reaching your objective may spoil some of the pleasure of your trek, but it could save your life or prevent your meeting up with a recreational accident. You *must* anticipate the strength of your party for the return trip. Weather could add to its complexity and delay your return.

Fire

The greatest threat to our forests is fire. Remote wilderness backcountry is usually limited to lookouts or other detection facilities, After the fall rains arrive, most fire lookouts are closed. However, forest fires do occur in late fall from time to time. Consequently, a small fire on a windy fall day often grows to a wildfire holocaust before it is detected. It is especially important that all users in brush and wooded areas be careful with fire. Before breaking camp, *be sure that your camp and warming fire is dead out! After striking camp, check again to be sure every spark is out!*

If campers are careless about fire, disaster can ensue.

If You Become Lost

You are lost if you do not see any landmark or terrain that you can positively recognize. There are still many areas in the wilderness where you might wander for several days without meeting another person or crossing a road.

The real danger you face if you are lost in the mountains is not man-eating bears or snuggling snakes but you yourself — if you panic. Panic, someone once said, "is when your heart is in your mouth, and your brains in your heels." Therefore, if you suddenly discover that you are lost, take it easy. Your first move should be to sit down and think. Retrace in your mind every step you have made from the last recognizable landmark up to your present location. Sitting and resting while you mull over your problem, you are conserving energy. By thinking things out, the mistake is usually remembered and the trail is found. Here are some hints that will be helpful if you can't figure your way back to a known landmark:

- Keep calm. Do not walk aimlessly. Trust your map and compass. Remember, without water you can last only two or three days; without food you can live two or three weeks or more.

- To find your position, climb to a place where you can see the surrounding terrain.

- If you feel that you just can't get reoriented, stay where you are, clear an area down to mineral soil, build a signal fire, and put green boughs on it. You will be found!

- Traveling down a canyon will usually lead you to a road or trail. (Great care should be taken when climbing around waterfalls found in many canyon bottoms, you may not be able to get back up!)

- Follow a road or man-made trail, for it will usually lead to some point of civilization.

- If you reach a telephone or power line follow it. As a last resort, follow a stream downhill.

- Before being caught by darkness, select a sheltered spot and make a bivouac camp. Stay in camp all night.

- A series of three whistles, three shouts, three shots or three flashing signals with a flashlight are universal distress signals. Use them only in an emergency!

Children on the Trail

The resilience of healthy children may amaze you. However, they do burn up a tremendous amount of energy and need to rest in the afternoon. Therefore, it is a good plan when you travel with small children to move camp only in the mornings and arrive at the new location just in time to eat lunch at the new campsite. Then the parents can settle down for a leisurely afternoon, while the small fry take a nap if they will.

Bring along a few rainyday games to keep your future heirs from becoming bored if they are "campbound" due to inclement weather. Let them help with camp chores, but don't send them out with a small camp axe to cut wood as I have seen parents do — with sad results. Cutting tools are not for kids. Teach them safety, and good manners, and you will be proud of them!

Everybody in the family can enjoy backpacking.

Children and Wilderness Hazards. Most youngsters like to explore, so parents should keep a watchful eye on them. Be especially watchful if you are camped by yourselves in a wilderness area. Never let the kids swim or wade alone in a lake or along swift moving water. Make them understand why they must not put their hands in holes, hollow stumps, or trees, why they must not pick up strange bugs. Tell them to stay away from snakes until they can be identified as harmless. Be sure that they can identify nettles and poison oak, ivy, and sumac. Until they are old enough to identify the edible and non-toxic kind, instruct them not to eat wild berries or plants. Keep an eye on them near campfires and teach them to leave matches alone! Explain to them that they must not pick up small animals or get between a wild animal and its young. Be sure to explain the reasoning behind these outdoor instructions rather than just, don't do it."

When the wilderness patrolling Ranger comes around on campground inspection or asks for your campfire permit, explain to the children why he does this and that he is their friend. Whenever you are in doubt or in trouble in the back country, you can call on the patrolling Ranger or recreational aide who covers the back country trails daily during the summer months and he will help you or advise you on what action to take.

Precautions for Adults and Children

Avoid rattlesnake country if possible and take maximum precautions against possible snakebite. Viper bites are more serious with small children than an adult because of size. A dose of viper poison (rattlesnake, copperhead or moccasin) goes further in a small body than a larger one. Usually, children are bitten about the body or face, and this can be far more serious and difficult to treat than a bite on a limb.

Most children today are under routine medical care and have been inoculated for tetanus. However, if they haven't already received tetanus shots, both parents and youngsters should be inoculated or be given a booster shot before leaving on a wilderness jaunt.

If any member of the family is allergic to insect stings such as honey bees and yellowjackets and other types of wasps, he should have anti-bee sting shots and one of the bee-sting syringe kits should be included in the first aid kit as an added safety measure. In all my years in the Ranger Service, I have only seen one case of dangerous bee sting and that was one of my trail crewmen who was allergic to bee stings. And the only snakebite happened to me when my horse bucked me off when a rattlesnake rolled down the steep trail bank between its legs and left me lying alongside the snake. In other words, there's little reason to fear the outdoors — but do respect it.

The Group Leader

Adequate, well-trained leadership is the best guarantee for the success of any wilderness jaunt. Too many well-intentioned businessmen and others take groups into the desert, to beaches, and into the woods and mountains without having had adequate experience to meet some of the emergencies that occasionally occur. Experience shows that one adult leader for every eight young people is desirable. *It cannot be emphasized too strongly that only leaders who are well trained in outdoor skills and first aid should consider assuming these responsibilities!*

Notifying Officials. As early as possible you should notify or contact the administrators of the area you plan to enter. Advise them of the size and average age of your group and outline your plans and itinerary. The leaders should be familiar with conditions in the territory to be visited. As stated earlier, maps are usually available from the U. S. Geological Survey, and recreational maps may be obtained from Park and Forest officials. Study them carefully and mark your route on them.

Know What to Do in Emergencies. Group leaders must make advance plans to cope with the unexpected. They should know:

- Whom to notify first in case of accident.
- Who will take charge if the leader is injured.
- Who will accompany an ill or injured hiker out of the mountains and home if he is able to walk out.
- Who is responsible for rescue, ambulance, and doctor bills.
- What to do if the group becomes separated.
- Where to seek help at intervals along the trail (from studying map).
- Where is the nearest phone, Ranger Station, pack station or road head — and what is the quickest and best route to get there?

Messages. When sending a message out for assistance, always write out the note. Include your name and unit, home addresses, phone number, age and address of injured person. Tell what happened, the condition and symptoms of the victim, exactly what is needed, and your exact location and amount of food on hand. Always send a party of two to deliver the message to make sure it reaches authorities.

The Shakedown Hike. A shakedown hike approximating the elevations and terrain to be encountered on the proposed trek should be taken before the main event. All persons should be required to make this hike, and all equipment should be taken along. In this manner, all members who are not physically able can be weeded out or plans can be changed to a less difficult outing. This is the time to test and eliminate unfit and excess equipment, to try out menus, and to become familiar with your pack and other gear — *don't* wait until you get out on the trail in the mountains, or the whole trip may have to be aborted.

Safeguarding Health. The first concern of parents when their children are engaged in an activity away from home is their health and safety. It must also be the first concern of the group leader. Recreation officials find that adults seem to get into more trouble than young folks! Most adults are not as prepared for strenuous activities as teenagers, so start conditioning yourself many weeks in advance. A thorough physical examination is a MUST if you plan on taking on the responsibility of leading a group of hiking backpackers! Check your pulse at home. It should be approximately 64 to 72 at rest and 100 to 105 when walking rapidly. Remember your normal rate — then when you reach higher elevations and your pulse gets above 130, you had better slow down — rest a bit and take it easier! Get into the habit of watching yourself, and those with you so as not to overexert. You have too much respon-

*Being a group leader is a serious responsibility —
not for the untrained or inexperienced.*

sibility to risk getting "knocked out." Remember, you
are out for a pleasure trip, and not an endurance race!

First Aid. Leaders of extended trips away from quick
transportation and medical treatment should prepare
themselves by completing at least the free Standard
American Red Cross First Aid Course, and preferably
the advanced course. Make sure the personnel and
group unit first aid kits are complete.

Many experienced groups carry prescription antibiotics, antihistamines, and pain killers when on extended hikes in remote country. Contact your family doctor for his recommendations regarding drugs, medicines, and vitamin pills to take along. Any member of the group having a history of asthma or other respiratory ailments should get medication and instructions from his doctor.

Pneumonia in high remote backcountry is a serious matter and not at all uncommon. The patient will have a high fever and his breathing will be rapid. The victim must have absolute rest, be kept warm and quiet, and receive medical attention as quickly as possible.

Chapter 12 takes up these and other aspects of First Aid more fully.

The Hiking Pace. Maintaining good "march discipline" is difficult when hiking with a group of backpackers. Many set too fast a pace so that the slower hikers end up scattered along the trail. Feeling rushed, those behind may attempt short cuts, with the chance of becoming lost or injured. When traveling with youth groups, an adult leader should always bring up the rear.

Travel only during daylight hours, and hold schedule to six hours of hiking or less per day. Ten miles per day should be maximum for young people with heavy packs. The packs should lighten a pound or two per day as food is consumed.

How far you can hike in a day will be regulated by your pace. Have the slowest person in the party up in front with the leader so that the group can walk at the pace this person can manage. Take short rest stops to enjoy the scenery and take pictures — you will enjoy these in later years. It's a good idea to look back over your trail. Study the way home, the trail will look different on the return trip! Play it safe, and mentally mark every fork at trail junctions so that you do not become confused on the return route. Observe nature's landmarks for future reference—stay found at all times!

A Last Word

A back-country outing is an inspirational journey — a lesson in respect for nature and its beauties. Properly planned, it will build character and physical fitness while developing self-reliance, resourcefulness, and a spirit of cooperation.

4

How to Outfit —
Knapsacks, Rucksacks and Packboards

Human Pack Horses

WHILE ON BACK-COUNTRY patrol, I have come across some painful sights: individuals and groups of tenderfoot backpackers loaded down like pack horses with about everything a sporting goods salesman could suggest. A large part of the gear was the kind only carried for auto and pack-train camping. Some were carrying their all in a side haversack knapsack that caused them to lean to one side; others carried suitcases or duffelbags on their shoulders, or slung crosswise on their backs with a rough piece of rope. On questioning a few of these dudes, I found that they had known no one to advise them regarding correct equipment or its cost. Others mentioned that their local library was too small to carry camping books, or that the books were all out on loan or that they couldn't afford to buy the books they wanted so had to compromise. I suggested to them several outdoor books, including the Sierra Club's excellent *Wilderness Handbook* or the *Boy Scout Handbook* for the kids (see the Bibliography). Most of those I talked with were still enthusiastic about backpacking — if they only could find some way to lighten their packs. Of course a few asserted that they had had it! They were through hoofing it — to use their expression. They would stick to wheels from now on.

After meeting a few of these unfortunate sore-backed sore-footed tenderfeet, the patrolling Ranger and the old-time backpacker think of their own honed-down lightweight packs in contrast: knapsack pack frame — 2½ pounds; sleeping bag rolled up in a bundle the size of a metropolitan Sunday newspaper — 3 pounds; plastic tube-tent — 1-pound; poncho — 1½ pounds; nesting one-man cook outfit — 2 pounds; freeze-dri and dehydrated food — 2 pounds per day; miscellaneous clothing and other gear, for a grand total of about 24 pounds, including a week's supply of food.

These packs are packed properly and carried in correct position.

Experience and Attitude

The difference between the experienced backpacker and the tenderfoot does not lie in experience alone. It is found in the difference of attitude. The old-timer doesn't select his equipment and gear on the basis of its good looks or interesting appearance or the sales pitch of the super-salesman in a sporting goods store, who is out to make a sales record. He considers carefully what function each item is to perform and checks off these functions against the piece of equipment. He also considers approximately how many times on a trip he will need or use a particular item and if it will be worthy of its weight.

One-Day Jaunts

For one-day trips, the matter is comparatively simple. About all you need to pack is: map of the area; guidebook; flashlight, compass, matches, small first-aid kit, snakebite kit (in season), insect repellent, rain garment if necessary, sweatshirt or flannel shirt, and a lightweight alpine rucksack in which to carry the gear. Not counting a canteen and lunch, this adds up generally to 2 pounds, yet you are prepared for the emergency that might occur. It is taken for granted that you have a pocket knife on you and a signal whistle.

Longer Trips

For longer trips, involving anything from a weekend to a tour of several weeks, you can still travel much lighter than you would have thought possible, thanks to the many new developments in the design of packs and their contents. The illustrations show packs and equipment for different kinds of trips of varying durations (Chapters 5 and 6 take up equipment and food in more detail), and several checklists to joggle your memory. None of these are the last word on what you should take, for no two individuals have the same needs and no two trips are alike either.

What Makes a Good Pack

The person who carries his food, shelter, and all necessary camping gear on his back has reached the ultimate in personal freedom to roam at will in the nation's wild areas. He can travel across country or over footpaths too rugged for saddle and pack stock to negotiate. Once the hiker has laid his plans and assembled his outfit, he can hike, hunt, fish, and rockhound to his heart's content; and in the most economical manner. But he can also become sore-shouldered, back-weary, and tired out by using the wrong size and type of knapsack — and by carrying it too far and too fast.

A never-ending argument goes on among outdoorsmen on the subject of what makes a good pack-sack. Before you get too far ahead in your planning, settle the question of what type of knapsack, rucksack, or packboard will meet your requirements for the hiking and camping season. If you already have a rucksack, decide if it fits all your needs or if you require one that will give you more hiking pleasure. Perhaps you will need two!

There are a considerable number of knapsacks, ruck-

WEEKEND TRIP

Rucksack	2 lb.	0 oz.	Gloves			9
Sleeping bag	2	8	Down Vest			8
Poncho	1	0	*Tube Tent		1	2
Ensolite		14	Food		4	0
*Miscellaneous Cord		2	Sun cream			2
*Pots & Miscellaneous	1	8	Hat			5
*Stove & Fuel	1	9	Rain Chaps			5
*First Aid		5	Total Weight: Leaving	17 lb.	7 oz.	
*Water Bottle		3	Returning 12 lb.	12 oz.		
Toilet Articles		3				
Spare socks		4				

*Community Property if two people are along: 2 lb. 6 oz. less.

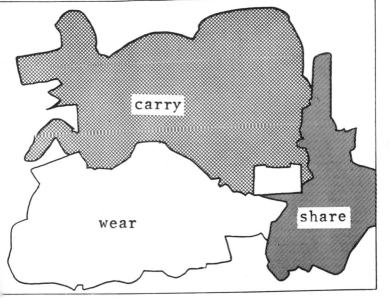

1-WEEK CLIMBING TRIP

	lb.	oz.		lb.	oz.
Backpack	3	8	*Carabiners	2	0
Rucksack	2	0	*Sling material	1	0
Ensolite		14	Toilet Articles		6
Sleeping bag	3	15	First Aid		5
Down Jacket	2	0	Sun cream		2
*Tent	4	8	Glacier Glasses		6
*Pots & Miscellaneous	1	12	Down Vest		8
*Stove & Fuel	2	8	Hat		5
*Water Bottles		6	Food	10	0
Spare clothes	1	8		50 lb.	14 oz.
Gloves		9			
Cagoule	1	6	*Community Property: Half	10 lb.	13 oz.
*Rope	8	0	Total Load: Going	40 lb.	0 oz.
*Pitons	1	8	Returning	29 lb.	13 oz.
Hammer & Holster	1	8			

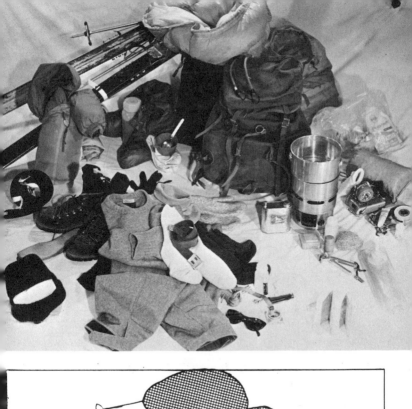

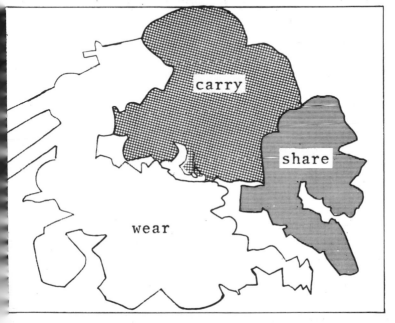

2-WEEK
PACK
TRIP

	lb.	oz.
Backpack and Frame	3	8
Sleeping bag	3	8
Ensolite		14
*Tent, poles, fly	4	4
*Pots & Miscellaneous	1	12
*Stove & Fuel	3	7
*2 Water Bottles		6
Personal cup (poly)		2
Toilet Articles		6
Spare clothes	2	0
Gloves		9
Down Jacket	2	0
Food (generous)	20	0
Knife		5
Miscellaneous Cord		2

	oz.
First Aid	5
Mosquito repellant	2
Hat	5
Flashlight (optional)	12
	44 lb. 11 o

*Community Property with two peop
Subtract half (4 lb. 15 oz.).

Returning less food and All f
(Less 23 lb.).

GOING:	Alone	44.11lb.
	Two	39.12lb.
RETURNING:	Alone	21.11lb.
	Two	16.12lb.

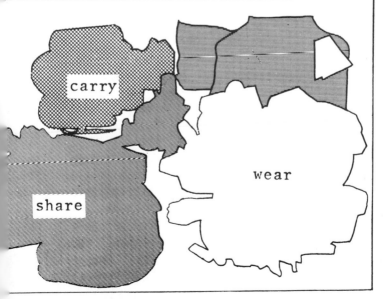

Packframe, bag, and contents laid out on plastic tube tent. At left, top, is pack frame and bag, at bottom is slimline down sleeping bag. In center, laid out on ensolite pad, at top are 2 Scout kettles behind stove. To left is famed Sierra Club cup. Next row, from left: knife, fork, spoon; water bottle; provision box; fuel container. Bottom row, from left: first aid materials, knife, flashlight, compass, match case. To right of pad, at top, are rolled-up downjacket, extra shirt and socks. Then, on poncho, are soap, toothbrush, toothpaste. Finally, nylon cord and grommet tabs for tent.
Courtesy The Ski Hut, Trailwise Equipment.

sacks, and packboards of various sizes, weights, shapes, types, and prices on the market today. Like other types of equipment, some are excellent, some are good and will do the job and some are only fair. You get what you pay for. Therefore, it is advisable to buy the best grade you can afford. It will serve you better and last longer and you will be better satisfied. When purchasing a new pack, keep these things in mind: What type of hiking or climbing will you be doing? Is the bag large enough or too large? How long will it hold up, considering what you will be subjecting it to?

The ski enthusiast spending a day on the ski slope will only need a small alpine pack to carry his lunch,

BACKPACKER'S CHECKLIST FOR ONE PERSON*

This list shows that you can backpack for a weekend with a total pack load of less than 17 pounds, or for an entire week with less than 25. Listed below are the equipment requirements for one person backpacking under relatively favorable summer conditions. The weight shown after each item indicates only how light it can be obtained. Your ability to achieve these low weights will be governed by such factors as weather, budget and personal requirements or preferences. Though you may find it necessary to add items to this list, each addition should be balanced most carefully, usefulness against weight. If traveling alone or into a very remote area, you will do well to plan for any eventuality. If a novice, your first trip should be brief and "educational."

	lbs.	oz.	
Packframe & packbag	2	15	(Max. 3 lbs. 11 oz.)
Sleeping bag	3	0	
Stuff bag (optional)	0	4	
Ground sheet	0	8	
Poncho or rain cape (optional)	0	12	
Camp rain protection	0	15	
Air mattress (optional)	1	2	
Extra clothing	2	0	
Cooking & eating equipment	1	0	(optionals not included)
Miscellaneous	1	8	(optionals not included)

Total with above optionals:	**14 lbs.**	**0 oz.**	

Cooking & Eating Equipment	Pocket knife	OPTIONAL:
	Spoon	Cookstove & fuel
	Polyethylene plastic cup	Additional cook pot
	Polyethylene plastic bowl	Wire grill
	Frying pan	**Poly. plastic shaker, pt.
	Cook pot, qt.	Fork
	Pot gripper or small pliers	Spatula

Miscellaneous:	First aid kit	OPTIONAL:
	Needle & thread	Snakebite kit
	36 ft. nylon cord	Canteen
	Sunburn lotion	Mirror
	Chap stick	Comb
	Mosquito repellent	Safety pins
	Matches	Candle (fire starter)
	"S.O.S." scouring pads	Sun glasses
	Toothbrush, toothpaste	Cap
	Toilet soap	Map
	Small towel	Compass
	Toilet paper	Pen-size flashlight

*Courtesy of Al Kelty of A. I. Kelty Manufacturing Company
**Can be used as canteen

KNAPSACK EQUIPMENT CHECKLIST FOR TWO PEOPLE

WOMAN

Qty	Item	lbs.	oz.
1	Knapsack	3	
1	Sleeping bag	3	
1	Foam pad	1	
1	Poncho	1	
1	Change of underwear		10
2	2 Prs. wool socks		6
2	Bandanna handkerchiefs		2
1	Hand towel		6
1	Pr. boot laces		1
1	Pr. camp moccasins	1	
1	BSA pocket knife		14
1	Flashlight, pen type		2½
1	Nested cook kit		4
1	Toilet kit	1	1½
1	Snakebite kit	1	2
1	Compass		1
1	Insect repellent		2
1	Waterproof matches		2
1	First-aid kit, small		2
1	Wool sweater		2½
1	Windproof parka		12
1	Army type sewing kit		12
2	Large face cloths		4
1	Roll toilet tissue		4
1	Food*	5	6
	Total:	**22**	**9½**
		lbs.	**oz.**

MAN

Qty	Item	lbs.	oz.
1	Knapsack	3	8
1	Sleeping bag	3	10
1	Foam pad	1	5
1	Mountain tent	2	9
1	Poncho	1	2
1	Change of underwear		10
2	Prs. wool socks		6
2	Handkerchiefs		2
1	Hand towel		6
1	Pr. boot laces		1
1	Pr. camp moccasins	1	2½
1	BSA pocket knife		4
1	Flashlight, pen type		1½
1	Nested cook kit	1	8
1	Toilet kit	1	1
1	Snakebite kit		4
1	Compass		2
1	Insect repellent		2
1	Waterproof matches		2
1	Wool sweater		14
1	Windproof parka		12
1	Map, topographic		1
1	Camera	2	
1	Fishing gear	1	8
10	Food*		
	Total	**33**	

*If dehydrated food is chosen carefully, 15 pounds should last a couple of hikers one week. The packs will, of course, weigh less and less as food is consumed each day along the trail.

camera, extra wax, small repair kit, and a few first-aid items. The ski mountaineer traveling the sky trails in the dead of winter will require an entirely different type of pack — one that is large enough to hold the camping and other equipment he needs to sustain him in high, cold winter terrain. Rock climbers and trail walkers need still other types of packsacks. Each has its own special use in the outdoors.

Regular backpacking trips usually require a frame and a bag; for extended trips or expeditions, a large bag is needed. Climbing bags should have an ice-ax carrier and a reinforced bottom. Check small things like zippers and buckles, straps, material, shape, weight (very important), and whether the pack is waterproof or just water resistant. Are strain points well reinforced? The Appendix gives the names of outfitters and their addresses. Those marked with an asterisk publish catalogs that you may send for to get an idea of the equipment, its weight and price.

Northwoods Packs. The woodsman in canoe country will need a large capacity pack such as the Duluth to transport bulky gear for comparatively short distances over portages. The Indian pack basket is also seen in canoe country, as well as along the Appalachian Trail in the East and in the Water Boundary Canoe Area. However, this type of pack is hardly ever encountered in the West, where the contour frame pack is most popular.

Packboards. In Alaska and other areas where freight backpacking is carried on in remote sections, the Alaska, Yukon, Trapper Nelson, and Army type packboards are used by guides and Indian packers. The Everest Himalayan Pak and bags are excellent alpine packs and are seen more and more along the high trails.

LAST-MINUTE CHECKLIST

This is a checklist only. **Don't take everything here.**

Taken by
1. **almost** everyone
2. Most
3. About half
4. A few

Knapsack	Pack Animal	TO WEAR OR CARRY	Approx. Wt. Ea. Article Ounces
1	1	Hat or cap	
2	2	Dark glasses	3
1	1	Shirt	6-16
1	1	Trousers or shorts	6-16
1	1	Belt	3-5
1	1	Shoes — boots	32-96
1	1	Socks	2-6
2	2	Bandana - handkerchief	1
1	1	Underwear	6-24
2	2	Maps (Toco or Forest Service)	1
3	3	Compass	3-5
1	1	Matches in waterproof case	1-3
1	1	Toilet paper	
2	2	Watch — cheap	2
1	1	Pocket knife — not cheap	2
1	1	Sunburn preventive	2
2	2	Insect repellent	1
1	1	Lip ice or lipstick	1
1	3	Knapsack or pack frame	16-64
1	1	Parka or jacket	16-34
2	2	Adhesive tape, moleskin, etc.	1
2	1	Raincoat, cape, poncho	3-24
1	1	Flashlight	3-9
1	1	Lunchbag, durable	1-2
1	1	Cup (2?)	4
1	1	Spoon	
2	1	Swim suit	3-24
2	2	Washing kit (self and clothes)	
4	3	Plastic lemonade shakes	3-6
4	-	Canteen or plastic bottle	6-12
4	3	Lemonade mix, soft drink mix	
5	5	Powdered coffee or tea or bouillon	
-	-	Water purifying tablets	
3	2	Fishing license	
3	2	Camera — Film	
-	1	Dunnage bag	24-48
2	1	Tarp or tent	16-96
1	1	Sleeping bag	36-176

*Courtesy of Robert K. Cutter, M.D.

LAST-MINUTE CHECKLIST

This is a checklist only. **Don't take everything here.**

5. Practically no one
? For consideration only

FOR DUNNAGE BAG OR KNAPSACK

Knapsack	Pack Animal	Article	Approx. Wt. Ea. Ounces
3	3	Inner bag	10-24
4	4	Outer bag	16-32
2	1	Ground cloth	3-32
3	2	Air mattress	32-82
5	4	Pillow or pad	3-12
5	4	Pajamas	14-16
1	1	Underwear (light) set	3-8
5	4	Undershirt (wool or quilted)	12
4	3	Under drawers (wool or quilted)	12
1	1	Extra socks	5-10
4	2	Camp shoes	6-32
3	2	Extra trousers	16-32
3	3	Hiking shorts	16
2	2	Shirts (lightweight)	6-12
4	3	Shirts, wool	16
1	1	Sweater, lightweight	8-16
4	2	Wool stocking cap or balaclava helmet	4
1	1	Bandanas	4
1	1	Powdered soap	4-8
4	2	Woolite or detergent	2
5	3	Sewing kit (small), safety pins	1
3	2	Extra optical glasses in case	3
5	3	Extra dark glasses in case	3
1	1	Flashlight (extra batteries, globes ?)	3-14
1	1	1/8" nylon or other cord	3-9
?	?	Kleenex (don't litter)	
?	?	Sanitary napkins	
5	2	Plastic wash basin	3-6
4	1	Collapsible plastic bucket	4
5	4	Cellulose sponge (small, thin)	2
?	?	Waterproof bags (strong) for camera, etc.	3
?	?	Small nail brush	1
?	?	Tickets, keys, money	
5	4	Mattress patching kit	
?	?	Clothespins, plastic	4
?	?	2 birthday candles or fire starters	1
?	?	Aluminum container (qt. filled)	39
-	4	Floves or mittens	3
4	2	Towel (diaper)	2
1	1	Thin plastic bags (ass'd), rubber bands	

Hikers traveling along the edge of an alpine lake in the High Sierra Nevada Range. Four styles of knapsacks are shown here (each pack averages 38 pounds loaded for one week's backpacking).

Note: all are carrying ice axes.

The Kelty Mountaineer Pack. Sleeping bag can be carried at bottom or top of pack. Courtesy Kelty Manufacturing Co.

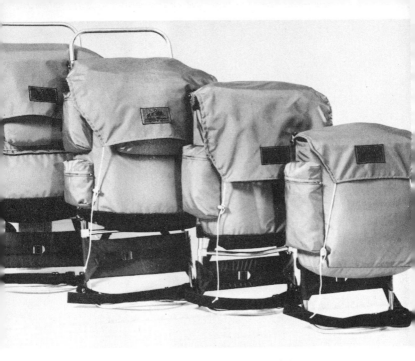

The adjustable Explorer frame pack, designed for a perfect fit. Courtesy Eddie Bauer Expedition Outfitters.

Packboards are good for what they were manufactured for — the lashing on of heavy, bulky, and odd-shaped loads that just won't fit in a knapsack or rucksack. The drawback in this case is that the lashed-on load has to be untied to enable one to get at the contents. This can become very annoying, in fact down right exasperating, especially if it is raining or snowing and you need something out of the pack such as a poncho, or lunch. The packframe that has the bag attached to it is a different matter. One can just raise the top flap and dig down for the needed article or zip open one of the outside pockets.

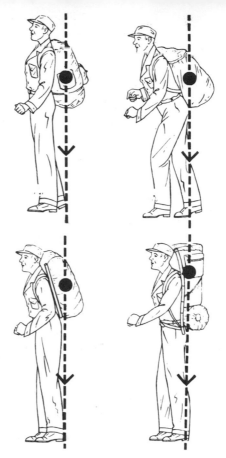

Top: Typical profile of the loaded knapsack and various rucksack-type packs. The weight of the short, bulky pack is concentrated low, away from the back. Its backward pull on the shoulders can only be overcome by an awkward leaning-forward position. Bottom: Usual packboard or packframe-type of pack. Weight is higher and closer to the back but still supported by the shoulders and back. Bottom: Long contoured frame brings pack weight still higher and closer to the back. Waist strap, anchoring frame to hips, transfers most of the weight to the hiker's hips and legs, where muscles are strong. Courtesy Kelty Manufacturing Co.

When selecting a knapsack, check it for size, strength, balance, quality and comfort, for this is one of the most important pieces of hiking equipment in your outfit. It must carry all your gear on your back with as much comfort and ease as is possible. Alpine Hut, North Face, Ski Hut, Gerry's, and other outfitters listed in the Appendix specialize in all types of alpine packs and packboards.

Rucksacks and Packframes. Most rucksacks are designed primarily for light loads and short trips. You can carry up to 40 pounds in some of the larger rucksacks, but for real comfort on the trail you should use a frame pack when you have a load greater than 30 pounds. Packframes are designed and constructed for greater comfort and durability. Firm, well-padded shoulder straps are standard equipment with the better frames. Several different sizes of bags are made for any type of knapsack hiking and need. At present, I am using the Kelty Mountaineer, which seems to ease my damaged back. (I have had my back fractured twice while in the Ranger Service over the past 36 years.) This pack was fitted properly and I have used it on treks into the back country of Alaska, down through Canada, and into Mexico on many jaunts. The comfort and efficiency with which you carry equipment into the mountains may well decide the success of your trip. Comfort and efficiency and fit are directly related to the design of a packboard or knapsack and also to how you pack it.

The Necessity of Pack Balance

The basis of hiking and climbing is balance — to keep the weight over the feet as much as possible. The average knapsack or rucksack places the weight low and away from the hiker's back. He must lean forward in an awkward posture to transfer the weight from his shoulders to his back. A packboard or frame allows the hiker to concentrate the weight higher and closer to his back. The contoured frame achieves this even more efficiently, transferring much of the weight to the hips by the use of a waist strap. (The illustrations demonstrate these points clearly.) However, a packframe may place the weight too high for comfort and agility if you have to do any steep climbing. Some models allow changing the position of the pack sack and the sleeping bag so that the sleeping bag is above in situations like this. And even with all the refinements, you may want to attach some foam rubber — about an inch thick and an inch wider than the strap — to the inside of the shoulder straps.

Packing the Bag

Design of pack is of no use if you do not pack your gear in the bag properly. The heavy items should be carried as high and close to your body as it is possible. Pack light things such as clothing, dried foods and sleeping bag, etc., at the bottom of your pack. Put heavier items at the top, such as your knapsack type stove, fuel bottle, cooking utensils, tent stakes, tarp or tent. Keep little things you want handy in the outside pockets or at the very top of your pack. Be sure that your first aid kit, lunch, and poncho are easily available. Toilet kit and other items should be put into waterproof bags so that the contents of the bag are not scattered. Food in one bag or bags, stove, etc. in another.

Learn how to hinch. First (a) hunch shoulders to lift the pack, then cinch the waist strap. Next (b) relax shoulders and let pack weight ride on hips. Note customary location of waist strap angling upwards and shoulder strap crossbar level with shoulders.

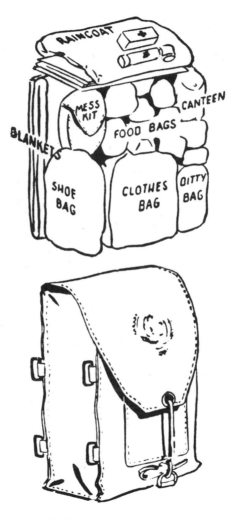

(a) How to pack a knapsack.

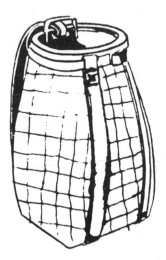

(b) How to pack a pack basket.

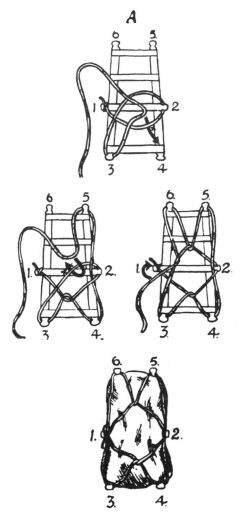

(c) How to pack a frame.

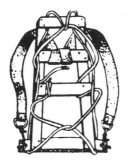 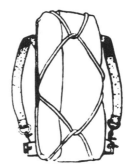

5

How to Outfit — Sleeping Bags, Tents, and Clothing

Hike-in Trail Equipment

WILDERNESS CAMPING IS easier today than ever before because of the new ultra lightweight tents, sleeping bags, knapsacks, stoves, and freeze-dri and dehydrated foods. Outdoor clothing is made lighter and stronger, too. Manufacturers are now making small knapsacks, sleeping bags, boots and other gear for women and the small fry. Whole families are now hiking into campsites that can't be reached by any other mode of travel. They are not only hitting the sky trails in the summer, but many are enjoying the new trend of snow and desert camping.

While hiking is among the least expensive forms of recreation, its enjoyment can be increased by moderate and judicious expenditures for well-built lightweight equipment.

The Importance of Sleeping Warm

About a third of the 24 hours is spent in bed or

along the trail in a sleeping bag. More campers have spoiled or aborted what could otherwise have been a wonderful camping experience because they couldn't get proper rest and sleep on cold nights. With proper guidance and the right bag, you can sleep warmly!

First consider the climate you are going to be in. If you are going to camp at high elevation in summer, you certainly will not need a double arctic sleeping bag. If you can only afford a lightweight feather bag and want to camp in the fall, you can always slip in a wool blanket and make out. The same can be done with the more economical celacloud and polyester fiberfills. Insulation thickness is what counts. If you intend to do some winter snow treking on skis or snowshoes, you will require a heavier feather bag. In this case if you own (as I do) a double arctic sleeping bag, you can use the 3-pound inner bag for desert and summer camping. But you may have to sleep in it with all your dry clothing at high elevations to keep warm, and use the inner and outer units together for snow camping.

Sleeping Bags

The sleeping bag is the single most important piece of camping gear — and usually the most expensive. Among the central considerations in selecting a bag are compressability, weight, and loft (the space between the inner cover of the bag and the outer).

A sleeping bag is for warmth and the thickness of the insulation determines the degree of warmth. It takes about a 1½ inch thickness of goose down to keep you warm at 40° F. and about ¼ inch of insulation for every 10 degrees the mercury drops. Whether the bag is filled with cotton, wool, kapok, or goosedown, 2 inches of one will keep you just as warm as 2 inches of another. In fact if it takes 2 pounds of down to make the 2 inches you won't be any warmer than if it takes only one pound. Why then pay for the very best grade (unless you can afford and want it) of prime white northern goose down in a sleeping bag? The answer is less bulk and weight!

All New Down. Down is the best insulation against cold provided by nature. Down feathers are the breast feathers of a duck or goose, which are very soft and warm. Down will hold air, retaining all body generated heat. It prevents cold and dampness from entering the inner bag. Air constantly circulates through the down filling, thus dampness on the inside is avoided. Down is waterproof and fire retardant.

Reprocessed down or second-hand materials, chicken feathers, and wool do not give off the same warmth, nor do they supply the same sleeping comfort as new filling.

Bags from Surplus Stores. If you decide to purchase a sleeping bag from a surplus store, be sure to inspect the bag carefully and see if you are getting just what you want. A tag on the bag will state what the contents are — wool, kapok, chicken feathers, etc. All good down sleeping bags are made with an overlapping or "box cell" construction.

The Outer Covering. An outer covering should be water repellent but not waterproof, for a sleeping bag must be able to "breathe." If this is not the case, the moisture from the body will be retained, thus causing the loss of warmth. Rubberized or waterproof covering on the bottom of bag causes the body to perspire unnec-

Ultralight mummy-type sleeping bag. Courtesy
Eddie Bauer Expedition Outfitter.

essarily, which may prove harmful to health; it will also
make your bag cold.

Polyester Fiberfill Bags. This type of bag is extremely
warm, fluffy, and resilient and is of non-matting material.
It is stronger and more lasting than kapok, wool, or
chicken feathers.

Celacloud Bags (acetate fiber). This bag-fill is more
resilient than kapok or wool, but not as warm or fluffy
as Dacron fiberfill. These bags are among the budget or
economy type and used mostly for summer outings.

Paired Bags. Double sleeping bags, which permit two
persons to sleep together, will be warmer than the same
bags used individually. However, this type is not recommended if one of the sleepers is restless and might keep
the other partner awake. If you wish to make a double
bed out of two single sleeping bags (bags must have

separate full-length L-shaped zippers), you should open each bag flat unzipping them completely. Place one bag on top of the other so that the bottom of each zipper will meet. Connect each zipper at the point at which they meet and proceed to zip together.

Sleeping Bags for Winter and Summer Backpacking. Naturally, a grade A goosedown bag is best for winter camping — and of course more expensive. If you do not care to pay for the price of one, do this: for zero weather camping, nest two summer bags by slipping one inside the other — and add a quilt or wool blanket if necessary. This is a particularly good arrangement if you intend to use your bags both in the warm summer months and for snow camping. A bag designed for zero or colder weather would be uncomfortable in milder seasons. I own a double artic bag. For summer jaunts, I use the 3-pound inner bag and during late fall and at high elevations, I nest the two — and have even added a blanket at times. I'm hard to keep warm!

Care of Sleeping Bags

Sleeping bags need a minimum of care and will last you a long time. Mine is over 20 years old and is just showing some color-fade on the outer covering from drycleaning. Here is a checklist of things to do for proper maintenance of sleeping bags:

- Sleeping bags should be aired out frequently. The sun's rays are an excellent sterilizer and will also help to refluff the filling.
- Bed sheets or liners should be used to keep the bag clean, and this will prolong its life.
- A *waterproof* ground sheet should be used under

the bag to protect it from moisture and wear. A 4½- by 8-foot sheet of 3-mil Vinyl is ample.

- If you rent your sleeping bag, turn it wrong side out and let it air in the sun. Insist on a clean bag sheet from the outfitter.

- Zippers should be handled carefully and slowly, otherwise they may jam or catch in the bag material and tear it.

- When the zipper is difficult to operate, apply soap or a coating of light lubricating oil the full length of the zipper.

- If the zipper becomes stuck — you may have to work it loose with a needle.

- Sleeping bags should be drycleaned for best results.

Tips on How to Keep Warm and Keep Your Sleeping Bag Dry

Don't add body moisture weight to your bag. In extreme cold temperatures, frost can add approximately a pound per day to bag weight — so beware!

- If because of cold, you pull your head inside the bag, it will frost up around the opening due to your warm breath. Breathe outside.

- You will sleep more warmly if you wear a knitted navy watch cap or a stocking cap on your head and wool socks on your feet.

- If your bag doesn't have shoulder protection at the opening, wrap a towel, sweater, etc. around your shoulders and neck to prevent body warmth from leaking out.

- Sleeping bags should be insulated from the ground — especially in snow country. Even if you use an air mattress, it should be protected by placing a ground sheet under it to keep moisture out and both the mattress and bag clean and dry.

- To keep frost from collecting inside your air mattress, it generally pays to blow it up with some type of lightweight air pump during the cold months — otherwise your damp breath will cause "icing" inside the mattress!

- The mattress should only be filled with air part way. I generally blow my bag up full, then lie on it and let air out until my body almost touches the ground. If you keep the bag fully inflated, it will be as uncomfortable as sleeping on the hard ground.

- During World War II, some mountain troops learned to sleep bare. I personally use a sweatsuit or a pair of wool long-john underwear that I keep just for sleeping.

- On water and snow surveys and ski patrols in the Ranger Service, I packed a rubber hot-water bag along. It was worth its weight when tucked into the bottom of my sleeping bag on cold frosty nights. Again, I could use the water in the bag for washing and cooking water in the morning and didn't have to use up precious fuel for melting ice or snow.

- I have also used a hand warmer inside at the

foot of my bag. However, the bag should be closed tightly at the neck, otherwise you are apt to smell and breathe fumes given off from the hand-warmer which could be toxic.

- You will sleep cold if you crawl inside your bag with the same clothing you hiked in during the day. Better sleep raw if you haven't dry clothing to put on.

Mattresses and Pads

Air Mattresses. For restful sleep in the high country, the go-light backpacker's air mattress will be one of the shorties or back packer models, 48 by 23 inches, weighing 1 pound 6 ounces sold by most alpine equipment dealers. (See the Appendix for names and addresses of outfitters.) For above timberline, recently, I have been using a Kelty 4-cell 11-mil vinyl plastic mattress, 22 by 46 inches inflated size. I have used it the past two years with very good results. (I carry a plastic repair kit, but haven't had to use it so far.) This item sells for only a few dollars.

Foam Pads. No lightweight down or other type fill bag can protect its occupant from heat loss to the cold ground, because the filling will compress under body weight. An air mattress does not insulate well because the air it contains is free to circulate and thus carry heat away from the body by convection. A pad of soft plastic foam provides more effective lightweight insulation.

Ensolite Pads. For the hardy sleepers who are willing to sacrifice the truly homelike comfort of a foam pad there is Ensolite, which costs just half as much as a foam pad. Backpackers generally use a ⅜-inch thickness for cold weather and on glacier-ice. For summer use, a ⅛-inch sheet adds negligible weight and bulk to the pack but makes a marked difference in sleeping comfort.

When hiking with burros, I go all out and pack a full-length 1½-inch polyurethane pad and enjoy its extra insulation and comfort. If you do not get proper rest on a mountain jaunt, your whole trip can be spoiled. Instead of coming home relaxed and refreshed, you arrive pooped-out and hate to go back on the job.

Mattress Care

Your air mattress should last you for many years if it receives proper care. Here are some hints on how to do this:

- *Do not* overinflate! A properly inflated mattress is quite soft.
- Blow it up full. Then lie on it and let air out until your body almost touches bottom. Overinflation will cause discomfort and excessive strain on the seams.
- Avoid contact with sharp objects. Look twice before placing the mattress on the ground. Always use a ground cloth (plastic or canvas) under the mattress to protect both mattress and bag.
- Do not inflate and leave any type of air mattress in the sun. Excessive heat causes air to

expand and may cause a blowout while you are out fishing or otherwise occupied.

- Don't use your air mattress for a float on an alpine lake. If it should spring a leak you might not reach shore. There have been some drownings due to cramps and cold shock in cold glacial lakes.

- If your mattress becomes wet for any reason, stand it up in an airy shady place to dry.

- Metal valve models: remove dust protector cap. Turn valve counterclockwise to open. Inflate slowly by mouth or pump until wrinkles and creases almost disappear. Take your time if at high elevation so that you do not provoke a nose-bleed! Close valve by turning clockwise until tight, and replace dust cap.

- Plastic valve models: There is no dust cap provided. Pull mouth piece stem out to open, push it in to close. Models with just a straight plastic tube, to close, fold tube back on itself and tie with a piece of string or close with a heavy-duty rubber band.

- Deflation and storage: To deflate, open valve and roll slowly from end opposite valve until all air is exhausted. Close valve and roll to convenient size. When storing for any length of time, keep in cool dry place either hanging or laid out flat, and with mattress half inflated. Do not ever store unless bag is completely dry.

- Never clean with gasoline! Use a bland soap and water.

Tents — Your Roof Overhead

To take a tent or not to — that is the backpacker's question. Naturally, a bed beneath the stars has a romantic appeal, but in most parts of alpine country it is best to be practical and carry some type of shelter. Along the Pacific Crest Trail in Washington and Oregon, one may find a few open-faced shelters. However, they are like those found off and on all along the Appalachian Trail, on a first-come-first-served basis. One especially needs protection from the elements on the Olympic Peninsula, where rainfall averages 12 feet per annum on the west side. There is nothing more uncomfortable than waking up to rain or snow in the face and a soggy sleeping bag.

Never believe anyone who tells you, "It never rains in August — or at night, or in the Rockies, eastern mountains or the High Sierra Nevada." It does rain during the day, as well as at night, in August, as well as every other month, even in California's Sierras. I have seen it occasionally rain for ten days straight, particularly when you are not expecting it. The success of a hiking jaunt may depend on adequate rain protection that will keep you warm, dry, and comfortable in the stormiest, drippiest weather — both while you're hiking and while you're in camp.

The Lightweight Hiker's Tent. This tent is designed for those who need complete protection from what is at times a hostile environment. The chief function of a tent is to prevent cooling by convection, i.e., movement of air. Not only must an effective tent seal its occupants from the elements, it must also keep the air inside the tent still. Therefore, a windproof outer shell is not

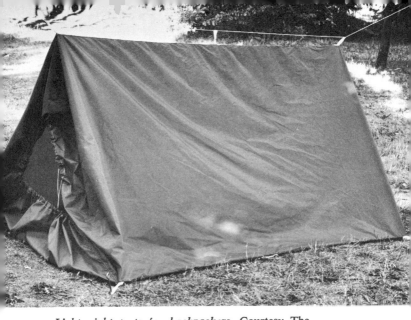

Lightweight tents for backpackers. Courtesy The Alpine Hut.

sufficient if it is pitched so loosely that the tent flaps violently in a wind and thus stirs up the air inside.

The more expensive knapsacker tent models weigh from 2 pounds up to 6 pounds. However, if a hiker is reluctant to purchase an expensive lightweight tent for the few times it will be used, he can tuck a plastic or nylon tarpaulin weighing between 1 and 2 pounds in any old corner in his pack. I might mention, however, that these tarps do not offer the privacy of a tent and will not stand up to heavy winds nor offer protection from insects. A point in their favor, is that they can be erected quickly and simply in so many circumstances that they will be more useful in wooded country than a completely secure mountain tent. A friendly reflected fire in front of the tarp-tent will keep you warm and help keep you cheerful.

The Plastic Tube Tent. This is more or less an emergency tent made of heavy gauge polyethylene, generally 8 or 9 feet in circumference and 9 feet long. It can be set up quickly into a tent with floor by inserting a nylon rope or heavy cord to form a ridge. Body weight anchors the tent. The weight runs about 16 ounces and the cost is minimal. Most outfitters carry them. Dr. Robert Cutter, an old friend and a man whose advice is *always* worth getting, advises against buying any with a circumference of less than 11 feet.

Clothing for the Trail

Don't take worn out old clothing into the backcountry. It just won't stand up! Outdoor clothing and footwear should be designed and selected for three main reasons: it must be strong, lightweight, and warm. It

The trail tent may be pitched in many different ways.

A tarp-tent is quickly set up.

should not bind or hamper your movements, and it should protect you from heat, cold, snags and dirt.

Some hikers and mountaineers like to hike in walking shorts. No doubt they are cool to wear in the summer during the day. However, nights are chilly or actually cold at the higher elevations. And shorts will give no protection to the lower legs. Many times I have noticed people in shorts with brush and rock scratches on their legs and a few badly sunburned, or with a rash from poison oak that was encountered on the way up from a lower elevation.

Dr. Robert Cutter, in his excellent outing equipment checklist (see Bibliography), gives you not only his own seasoned advice on clothing and other items but the feedback from readers, who don't always agree with his pronouncements. He suggests for a two-week trip: one or two lightweight shirts plus one wool shirt (not scratchy — long sleeved, pockets that fasten); one or two pairs of trousers (jeans are popular but western type are often too tight — industrial type cut loosely preferred by some — army surplus fatigue pants by others); hiking shorts, with a leather seat patch, if you like them; long underwear in cold climates; rain poncho or rainproof jacket and pants.

This checklist also reminds hikers of all the small personal items that can make a trip enjoyable rather than a series of discomforts — such necessities as soap, sunburn preventive, hat, first-aid supplies, sewing kit, flashlight, and other useful but easy-to-forget things such as a plastic bag big enough to fit over your sleeping bag.

Dressing to Keep Warm. The Gerry Company, well known manufacturer of outdoor equipment, offers the following general observations on clothing to keep warm.

Your body burns food to produce from 2400 to 4500 calories of heat a day and about two pints of water in the form of insensible perspiration. To keep warm, heat must be conserved and water vapor carried off without passing into the clothing layers. How do you get rid of two pints of water without it soaking into your clothing? Ventilation is the answer! Successful ventilation requires two conditions: first, there must be space next to your skin for air to circulate; and second, air must be free to enter your clothing, usually at the wrists and pants, cuffs and waist — and leave at the neck. Genuine net underwear with holes larger than ¼" will take care of the ventilating layer. Avoid underwear that clings to your skin and wicks the moisture into your clothing.

The next layer consists of more or less conventional clothing: the wool shirt, the heavy trousers. Prime considerations here are comfort, utility, and durability. Wool or some of the new synthetics in a spun fiber are good because they don't mat down and they stay warm when wet.

The insulation is your most important layer, and the most important thing to remember about insulation is thickness. Actually, dead air does the insulating and any material that will stop the circulation of air inside your clothing will be effective insulation. It could be steel wool or the best grade of down. Down is an ideal insulator for two good reasons: one, to insulate a certain thickness requires fewer ounces of down than any other material; and two, it is much more compressible. . . .

To keep the weather out of your insulation, you need a windproof, water repellent outer shell. Sometimes this is provided in the outer covering of the insulating jacket, but more commonly it is supplied by an outer wind parka capable of being completely sealed around wrists and face. If the wind is allowed to penetrate the outer layers of your insulation, it reduces the effective thickness. Rainwear also belongs to this category when there is danger of your insulation becoming wet.

Emergency Equipment

Every so often newspapers carry stories of men, women, and children who have been trapped in the outdoors, prevented by injury or weather or other circumstances from returning to civilization. While such difficulty represents a ten-million-to-one shot for the average camper, it is well to consider the elements of survival before venturing into the back country for an extended period of time. First, different conditions offer different necessities: in the desert, one must have water; in frigid climates, staying warm is what counts; in all situations, food and shelter are basics.

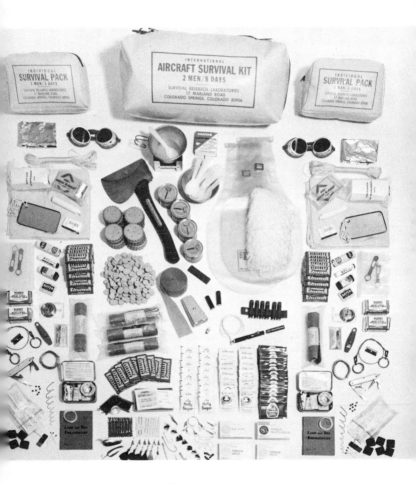

If you fly into a wilderness area to start your hiking jaunt, this is an excellent kit to have in the plane or along on a pack trip. Courtesy Survival Research Laboratories.

I	**II**	**X**	**F**	**≫**	**K**
Require doctor — serious injuries	Require medical supplies	Unable to proceed	Require food and water	Require firearms and ammunition	Indicate direc and procee
↑	**I⟩**	**⌐⌐**	**△**	**LL**	**L**
Am proceeding in this direction	Will attempt to take off	Aircraft badly damaged	Probably safe to land here	All well	Require fuel and o
N	**Y**	**ЛL**	**W**	**□**	**!**
No — negative	Yes — affirmative	Not understood	Require engineer	Require compass & map	Require signal lamp

GROUND TO AIR EMERGENCY SIGNAL CODE

INSTRUCTIONS: 1. Construct symbols in a north-south direction to obtain best shadows **2.** Make symbols at least 30 feet long, if possible. **3.** Tramp symbols in snow, cut or burn i vegetation, dig in ground, form by lines of rocks or brush, or construct by any other mean which will produce contrasting patterns.

Emergency signals are a good thing to know.

Now, if a camper had a string of porters behind him, he'd have no trouble taking along all of the equipment needed for all conditions. The typical camper carries his kit on his back, however, so weight is a prime consideration. In the photograph are two survival kits produced by the Survival Research Laboratories, 17 Maryland Road, Colorado Springs, Colorado 80906. The contents of these packs indicates what the experts think is basic emergency equipment. The small, 1-man, 3-day kit includes goggles, reflector paper, rope, meat bars, chocolate bars, mirror, soap, candle, bandages, rescue blanket, pocket first aid kit, wire snare, razor blade, knife, insect repellent, sun stick, water-purifying tablets, aspirin, booklet, fishing line and hooks, matches, shrill whistle, flint, signal flares. The larger, 2-men, 8-day pack also includes mini-stove, dry fuel, pot and spoons, hardtack, canned pemmican, woodsman's saw, and instant coffee-with supplies. Of course, it is not essential to purchase one of these kits. What is necessary is that the think-ahead hiker have some of this basic survival equipment along in his backpack whenever he goes far from civilization, where it is impossible to look for help to anyone except himself.

Keep in mind the basics — food, clothing, and shelter — as they relate to the particular environment you're in, and you should have no problems. Wood for a fire and for some kind of shelter, pure, fresh water, fish and game, wild fruits, nuts, and vegetables are some of the things you can take from your natural surroundings. Be careful. Don't panic. Think out all of your moves carefully, and you'll be home free.

6

Going Light with Freeze-Dri and Dehydrated Foods

Why You Eat More on a Hike

THERE IS SOMETHING about the outdoors that whets the appetite. No doubt it is the invigorating zip of the clean fresh air at higher elevations, free from fog and smog of our large cities, plus the exercise of packing into wild country.

The observation that an army travels on its stomach can be extended to the backpacker too! How far you can travel and how long you can stay is limited by the amount of food and gear you can carry comfortably on your back. But recent developments in lightweight foodstuffs and equipment have increased the amount that you can carry to an astounding degree compared to possibilities only a few years ago.

Food for the Hike

With careful planning, knapsackers can, and should, get by with 1½ to 2 pounds of food per person per day.

Many basic deyhdrated food items can be purchased at your local supermarket, and several firms specialize in packaging foods for the backpacker. All dehydrated foods should be tried out at home or on the shakedown hike before they are used on extended trips. Generally, I have found that if you soak the food a little longer than called for in the directions and cook it slightly longer the flavor is better and it is more tender.

Knapsack campers must have proper balance of proteins, carbohydrates, and fats. Don't depend on catching fish to add to the menu, fish can be elusive. Your menu should be complete without them, or you may go hungry.

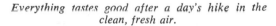

Everything tastes good after a day's hike in the clean, fresh air.

About Menus

Menus satisfactory to all members going on the hike should be worked out well in advance. Even experienced groups tend to make their menus too complex for backpacking. Simple, tasty, and nourishing meals can be easily prepared in aluminum saucepans in little more time than it takes to boil water.

To save time, I put the dehydrated food to soak immediately on arrival at my campsite. By the time I have pitched my tarp or tent and gathered firewood, the soaking food is ready to cook. Bacon and eggs (unless you use dehydrated bacon bars and powdered eggs), pancakes, and frying pans are luxuries that most experienced knapsackers leave at home. High-protein cereals make more efficient breakfasts for backpacking.

Here is a sample seven-day food supply for one person (courtesy of Colin Fletcher):

7	pkg. dried fruit (apple, date, peach, cocktail)	1 lb. 13 oz.
8	pkg. dried soup (mushroom, ham and pea, asparagus, egg macaroni, oxtail)	1 lb. 7 oz.
5	bars meat food	1 lb.
2	bars bacon	7 oz.
4	pkg. dried potatoes	1 lb. 9 oz.
1	pkg. dried beans	8 oz.
1	pkg. dried vegetables (onion, spinach, cabbage)	4 oz.
	Powdered milk	1 lb.
	Granulated sugar	1 lb. 8 oz.
	Mixed dry cereal	1 lb.
	30 tea bags	3 oz.
	3½ bars mintcake	1 lb. 6 oz.
	Dry raisins	1 lb.

Salt	3 oz.
1 bar rum fudge	8 oz.
Gross total (wrappings, etc.)	14 lbs. 3 oz.
Average daily gross	2 lb. ½ oz.

Improvements in the Eating Line

There has been a great improvement in the past decade in food preservation by vacuum-drying and quick-freeze methods. Out of this has emerged a whole new food-supply industry catering to the outdoorsman. New "instant" and "quick-freeze" dried foods are being prepared in individual and group-size meal packets. For example there are 1-man, 2-man, 4-man, and 8-man units that can be used in various ways: 1-man for 8 days, 8-men for 1 day, etc., whatever suits your particular need.

Below are some sample menus specially developed for wilderness travel (courtesy of Chuck Wagon Foods):

BREAKFAST

Egg Pancake Mix	Prunes
Pancake Syrup Mix	Wheatoata
Shortening	Milk for Cereal
Oatmeal	Tea, Sugar
Milk for Cereal	Sugar Packets
Hot Chocolate	Bolton Biscuits
Sugar Packets	Jelly Packets
Scouring Pad	Scouring Pad
(in plastic bag)	
Toilet Tissue	Toilet Tissue
(in plastic bag)	
Plastic Mixing Bag	Plastic Mixing Bag

Ralston
Milk for Cereal and Drinking
Sugar Packets
Shortening
Bolton Biscuits
Spanish Omelet
Salt and Pepper
Scouring Pad (in plastic bag)
Toilet Tissue (in plastic bag)
Plastic Mixing Bag

LUNCH

(Hot Lunch)	(Cold Lunch)
Chicken Consomme	Bolton Biscuit
Macaroni and Cheese	Deviled Ham (Can)
Fruit Drink (Crystals)	Fruit Drink (Crystals)
Bolton Cookies	Plastic Knife
Afternoon Snack:	Folding Can Opener
Milk Shake	Afternoon: Apple Slices

Beef Bouillon
Vegetable Dinner with Rice
Hash Brown Potatoes
Chocolate Malted Milk
Afternoon: Raisins

DINNER

Chopped Beef and Spuds	American Chop Suey
Shortening (for Frying)	Spinach
Sliced Apples for Stewing	Butterscotch Pudding
Bolton Biscuits (pre-baked)	Bolton Biscuits (pre-baked)
Fruit Drink (Crystals)	Milk

(Baking Menu)

Vegetable Broth	Fudge Cake Mix
Spaghetti and Tomato Sauce	Baking Cups
Bolton Biscuit (pre-baked)	Milk

Evening Drink: Hot Chocolate

Wet-pack Versus Dri-pack

Each camper will have to decide for himself what he considers to be a reasonable compromise between necessity and pure luxury. Canned goods are too heavy to be packed in any appreciable amounts, nevertheless, canned items can break the monotony of too many starchy foods. A few small cans of fruits, tomatoes, or a can or two of your favorite vegetables will be helpful if you have an animal to tote the load — otherwise it will pay to stick to the backpacker's menus.

Get Acquainted with the Dehydrated Food Outfits

No doubt most of us are familiar with food industry names like Wilson, Kellogg, and General Mills. But how many know the people who cater to the knapsacker and other go-light campers: Dri-Lite, Bernard's Food Industries (Kamp-Pack), Chuck Wagon, Stow-A-Way? Anyone who spends at least part of each year living out of doors, away from supermarkets and civilization, should become acquainted with these firms. The people behind these companies are usually outdoorsmen themselves and they recognize the needs of the sportsman — Roy Walholm of Survival Research Laboratories, Bill White of Stow-A-Way, Dr. Frank Bernard of Kamp-Pack, and Ann Benedict of Dri-Lite, to name a few.

Write for the food suppliers' catalogs (addresses are

FOOD LIST FOR BASE CAMP
TO BE PACKED IN BY PACKER
4 PERSONS---10 DAYS

MEAT
- Ham ....6 lbs.
- Bacon — 1 piece ....6 lbs.
- Pork and beans..................4 cans
- Spam, etc. ....5 cans
- Corned beef ....5 cans
- Fresh meat
- Soup ....5 cans
- Shortening ....5 lbs.
- Butter ....5 lbs.
  (Margarine keeps best)
- Eggs (in ctns.) ....6 doz.

VEGETABLES - FRUITS
- Potatoes - fresh ....20 lbs
  (or cans of dehydrated)
- Onions ....5 lbs.
- Corn ....3 cans
- Peas ....3 cans
- Fresh vegetables
- Oranges ....2-doz.
- Lemons (or juice)................½ doz.
- Fruit juices ....10 cans
- Fruit - whole ....6 cans
- Fruit - cocktail ....4 cans
- Raisins ....4 lbs.
- Dried fruits ....3 lbs.
- Jam ....3 jars
- Peanut butter ....1 jar
- Pickles ....1 jar
- Wax paper ....2 rolls

CEREALS
- Pancake flour ....5 lbs.
- Cornmeal ....4 lbs.
- Crackers ....5 lbs.
  (some hardtack)
- Bread ....12 loaves
  (uncut keeps best)
- Cookies - mixed ....5 lbs.
- Rice ....1 lb.
- Breakfast foods
  (1 ctn. misc.)

GENERAL
- Milk - small ....12 cans
- Salt ....1 lb.
  (More if hunting)
- Pepper ....1 can
- Sugar - white ....5 lbs.
- Sugar - brown ....1 lb.
- Tea ....½ lb.
- Coffee ....5 lbs.
- Syrup ....½ gal.
- Vinegar ....1 pt.
- Salad Oil ....1 pt.
- Chocolate bars ....2 boxes
- Soap - toilet ....2 bars
- Soap powder ....1 box
- Candles ....6 each
- Matches ....2 boxes
- Paper towels ....2 rolls

Fresh meat for first day or so can be taken in frozen solid and well wrapped in newspapers and canvas.

Fresh vegetables can be freshened in camp — root types buried in wet soil — lettuce, etc. in wet cloths.

Bisquick or similar bread and cake mixes should be added if a Reflector Oven or Dutch Oven is taken along.

For more than 10 days or more than 4 people (don't forget the packer), increase amounts in proportion — some condiments, salt, pepper, etc. in lesser ratio.

COOKING EQUIPMENT

Grate or grill for camp fire
3 Kettles with covers, bails
1 Coffee pot
2 Fry pans
1 Griddle, cast iron
   or lighter metal
4 Plates
4 Bowls
Water bucket
   (Canvas is best)
Butcher knife

Cook's fork
Mixing spoon
Mixing - Serving bowls
Pancake turner
Can opener
Table knives, forks
Teaspoons
Serving spoons
Dish towels
Dish cloths
Scour pad

in the Appendix). They are in the business to fill your pack, chuck-box, saddle bags, kyack, aircraft or boat galley with excellent food values. Several of these outfits also provide survival food and water kits for our military forces, Civil Defense, and for the outdoorsman.

Most of these dishes are practically "instant" and none take longer than 15 to 20 minutes to prepare. With water added, they will make up to 1½ to 2 pounds of processed food per person and their average calorie count is 3,000. Some products can be kept stored up to five years or more.

My own experience with the new products on the trail (and aboard my boat) has shown me that they are what the companies claim them to be and they do what they promise. Of course, tastes differ and if you are a fussy eater, you should cook and taste-test some of the items offered from the various dehydrated food companies before heading out on the trail too far from a supermarket.

Some persons have a dietary problem and are limited in their selection of foods. Some become constipated as a result of the sudden change from home-cooked food to highly concentrated food; so be sure to add plenty of dried fruit to the menu. Planning menus and making up provision lists for an anticipated trip into the back country can be fun, but plan wisely!

Hiking with Donkeys

Knapsackers who use pack stock seldom restrict themselves to the menu of the backpacker. Why should they when the food (and most of the gear) can be packed on a broader and stronger back with four legs to support the load? Nevertheless, a pack trip should still be a go-light proposition. If you want to take your "home" with you on what is to be a strictly "camping" experience, you must remember your responsibility for the care of the hired stock and the fact that the animals represent an extra cost. Additional weight means more pack animals to be found each morning, to be loaded and unloaded, and to kick up more dust along the trail.

Hints on Preparing and Cooking Dehydrated Foods

1. Replace water as it boils down. Water evaporates very rapidly at high elevations, for instance, so in order to keep water content sufficient for absorption of dry contents plus absorption loss, extra water may be added.
2. Increase the soaking time, and soak in warm water whenever possible.
3. Increase simmering time, but cook slowly. Flavor and texture improve with long slow cooking.
4. Keep cooking containers covered. This will help retain both moisture and heat. Remember to watch dishes that will tend to boil over and to stir foods like starches that tend to stick to the bottoms of kettles.

Food Storage and Cleaning Up

As a rule, campers who keep a clean camp and use a minimum of odorous foods are less bothered by animals than those who allow garbage to collect. However, any food or food container that emits an odor is a natural attraction for animals. Food left lying around or in open boxes is a definite invitation.

Avoid storing food on the ground or in your tent. Back-country campers often suspend their supplies between two trees, out of reach of bears. Use clean wrapping material or airtight containers, and keep the food as cool as possible.

Rangers request that you burn and bury all garbage and food wrappers and containers, including foil and cans. Burning removes the food scent and animals are not so likely to dig up the remains. Be considerate of other outdoorsmen — leave a clean camp. Our camp sites, trails, streams, and lakes are becoming unsightly from litterbugs and thoughtless persons throwing or dropping the foil wrappers from gum, candy, and food. Recreational agencies cannot emphasize this point enough. Some hiking clubs require their members to pack out all empty cans, foil, and bottles. These sportsment and woodsmen are to be commended.

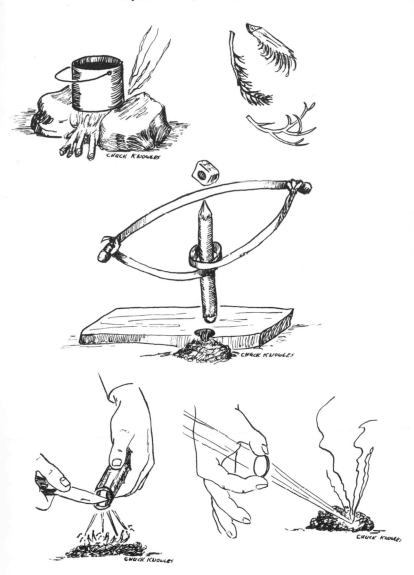

7

The Technique of Hiking and Foot Care

Getting Off on the Right Foot

WHEN HIKING, USE the "Indian technique" and you will have a lot more energy at the end of the day's hike! Adopt a gait that allows you to breathe normally. Point your toes straight ahead or slightly in. Coming down lightly on your heel now reach forward with your foot and push up off your toes. With a little practice you will acquire the swinging gait used by the Indians and northwoods guides. This swinging trail pace will eat up the miles. Learn from past experience to set a pace that you know you can keep all day long with a minimum number of rest periods. In my own trail experience, I find that more short rest stops get me to where I want to go than do fewer, but longer, breathing spells. To save time, I lean my pack against a tree or sit on a rock or log with the pack resting against the object. This saves the chore of removing and rehoisting the load back and forth on my back. For the longer stops, of course, remove the pack.

Adjust your pace to the weight and distance you

must tote your pack, so that you arrive at your destination early with enough pep and energy to pitch a safe and comfortable camp. Two miles an hour is a satisfactory gait when backpacking.

How to Hike Rough Terrain

When traveling in mountain country, hiking up or down hill can be made easier by turning your boot slightly sideways to brake for firmer footing.

A good method when climbing steep terrain is to climb about a thousand feet an hour at a pace that allows you to reach the crest of a ridge or peak without being short of breath. When hunting, this is important! If you top a ridge and sight game but are panting hard, you will be unable to hold a steady aim.

The Importance of Proper Foot Care

The novice or occasional hiker doesn't always realize the importance of foot care. In fact, the foot probably receives the least care of any part of a person's body. The back country hiker cannot afford to neglect his feet! Many vacationers fail to realize that good old "shank's-mare" must get you to your destination, after you leave the road end, and all the way back again to your car. Many of us have lost the art of walking while we earn a living in the concrete canyons of the cities. Several times while patrolling remote wilderness country, I have dismounted to let some misguided, foot-sore hiker ride my horse while I led him back to his camp.

It is this type of rocky trail that is rough on shoe leather. It pays to wear the best kind of hiking boots — a pair that will get you there and back home again!

Wrong Sock and Boot Combination

In most cases, the victims of sore feet wear the wrong sock and boot combination. Some leave home with shoes or boots too old and worn, too small, for feet swell while hiking, or with new boots that had not been properly broken-in for rugged mountain scrambling. In several instances, I have even had to use my horse shoeing outfit to repair a hiker's boots that had lost a heel or to pull nails that were forcing their way into the inside of their boots. (This has happened to me too.)

How to Prepare Your Feet for Backpacking

Your feet should be toughened weeks before the treks on long, back country trails. You can start to get them, and the rest of your body into condition by walking at every opportunity that presents itself. Try to lengthen your walk a little each day by stepping off an extra block or two. Knock off 10 or 12 miles a day on the weekends, if possible. When you start this hardening-up exercise, wear the socks and boots you plan to use on the proposed trek. (I know several executives who wear their boots to the office when preparing for a trip of this sort.)

If you are an office worker and your place of business isn't too far off, walk to work! At least walk part of the way. Hike up the steps instead of using the elevator. A city friend of mine hardens up before a knapsack trip by loading up his knapsack with about 40 pounds of books and then hikes down the front steps of his seventh floor apartment and back up the rear steps twice a day.

If your feet perspire considerably, use a foot powder in the morning when you don your socks. Before retiring, soak your feet in cold water, dry and massage them with witch hazel or alcohol. Trim your toenails almost straight across, rather than rounded to the shape of your toes. This will prevent the corners from cutting into the skin.

In any event, wash your feet at least every night while out on a hiking trip and *change socks every day*. When the trail has been steep and going has been rough, it is refreshing to stop along the way when possible and bathe your feet in a cold mountain stream or lake. However, be sure to let your feet cool off first before dunking them into cold water. Otherwise, they may blister!

Beware of the Sock You Wear

When fitting inner or outer socks, *make sure* that all wrinkles and creases are smoothed out, or you will get into real foot trouble! Don't ever start on a hiking jaunt wearing old socks that have been darned, or socks that are of rough texture or have holes in them. They will cause sore feet, something you can't afford to have out on the trail far from home and medical care. Always wear new socks when taking off on the trails!

For foot comfort, wear a light pair of wool socks and over them a heavier pair a half-size larger. The extra pair will help cushion the feet when you're hiking over rough terrain. For the hiker who cannot tolerate wool, a pair of cotton or nylon stretch socks with fleeced cushioned soles will serve. They are inexpensive and can be purchased at most surplus stores.

Watch Those Tender Spots

At the first sign of a tender spot *anywhere* on your feet, be sure to stop *immediately* and tape the spot carefully before it turns into a blister. Blisters are not only painful to hike along with, but they can become infected if not treated properly and may cause serious complications when you're a long way from the road-head. If you do blister your feet, good judgement indicates that you abort the trip and head for home. See Chapter 12 for treatment.

Some foresighted hikers, who know they have a tendency to blister, tape the sensitive spots *before* they start out. A stretch adhesive bandage that is available in up to 4-inch widths is excellent for this purpose, as it can be smoothed onto the foot and ankle without wrinkles and it stays put.

Wash Those Socks. Actually when the going is hot and tough, and you are sweating considerably, it is a good idea to change socks once or twice along the trail if time permits. Hang the damp socks on the outside of your pack frame and they will dry rapidly in the sunlight and breeze.

After the camp chores are done at night, wash the socks you hiked in during the day in lukewarm soapy water, rinse, and gently squeeze reasonably free of moisture (do not wring). Stretch them back into their original shape and dry them slowly, but not too close to your camp fire. If they are not completely dry before you retire for the night, you can hang them from your pack so they dry while you travel along in the morning. Don't take wet or damp socks, or in fact any damp clothing, into your sleeping bag to dry as some writers suggest. This will just add moisture to your bag — something you do not need! If it is raining or wet outside, and you must dry socks or clothing inside, place the articles between the ground cloth and your air mattress. If they are not completely dry by morning and you haven't any other dry sock in your outfit, don the damp ones and they will dry on your feet en route to your next destination.

Boots for Hiking

There is no such thing as an all-around shoe or hiking boot that will do for all types of terrain and weather conditions. Ideally, you should select the type and kind of boot for the terrain to be traveled, but this is obviously impractical in many cases. In any event, the boot should be correctly fitted, and have strong counters, soft uppers, and rugged lug soles. The boots should be fitted over two suitable pairs of socks with plenty of room to allow your feet to spread under the weigth of a pack load. They should have ample room in front for your toes to spread naturally and comfortably, but they should hug the arch and heel snugly for support and to prevent friction. A boot or shoe that is loose in the heel will cause slipping and, in turn, blisters. If your heel is loose in the boot, it will generally wear out a pair of sock heels within a day or so.

Lacing Your Boots. For good circulation and foot comfort, it is suggested that you lace your boots snugly over the first four eyelets, then tie a square knot.

A lightweight hiking boot weighing under 3 pounds. Courtesy Eddie Bauer Expedition Outfitter.

All eyelets or hooks above this should be laced more loosely. If you lace your boots too tightly, it will cause your feet to swell and become numb or cold.

If you purchase boots that lace with hooks instead of eyelets, be sure to get the large-hook type that are of brass or non-tarnish metal. Some types of hooks on shoes catch in brush, etc., and are forever breaking off.

To keep dirt and other debris out of the top of your boots, wear your lower pants legs outside. Cut off and remove cuffs. All cuffs do is collect debris along the trail.

About High Boots. High boots are heavy, restrict circulation in the lower legs, and are unnecessary, unless you are in heavily infested snake country. Trousers of tough material will protect the legs sufficiently from brush and insets. Rattlesnakes and other vipers, if they strike at all, seldom hit above the ankle.

Types of Soles. Probably the nearest to an all-around hiking shoe is the Army's Munson Last or the military

Two pairs of camping and trail boots with Vibram lugged soles. The hightops are Browning, the low ones are of European make.

combat boot with lugged soles. If you happen to be hiking with pack stock, a leather boot offers more protection in case a pack animal accidently steps on your foot.

Hob-nailed, cleated Vibram soles have a distinct advantage if there is much snow to travel over in high mountain passes, or when crossing large stretches of wet mossy terrain. Hob-nailed soled shoes or boots will slip on smooth rock and can prove dangerous at times. Nail-studded soles require more skillful maneuvering on smooth rocky terrain and the hiker must ever be alert that he doesn't slip and take a nasty fall.

Probably the best compromise for summer and fall mountaineering is the Vibram sole, consisting of long-wearing composition cleats or lugs, mounted on a light-weight hiking boot. For general pleasure hiking, I have found some military mountain boots too heavy. So far as I am concerned, I have found the same goes for the extra heavy (and strong) military ski boot! The Vibram sole is ideal and holds very well on rock or swampy or grassy slopes; if you are careful, it will hold on mossy rock, but *beware* of smooth wet rock or wet roots or leaves! This same sole holds well, too, on snow that is not too hard-frozen. However, when I get into that type of terrain, I don crampons for safety reasons.

Avoid smooth leather soles at all costs — they offer no traction on pine needles and grass and are dangerous in most terrain. The experienced hiker doesn't fear the outdoors, he just practices safe procedures and uses common sense. He doesn't want to suffer a sprained ankle or broken leg while out on a pleasure jaunt!

The Viet Nam Combat Boot. This heavy-duty light-weight boot with cleated rubber soles and heels, grips the ground under most conditions. The black leather toes and heels, which are vulcanized to cotton-nylon O. D. uppers combine light weight with rugged strength. They are sold at many surplus stores for around $8.95.

Cold Weather Boots. All-rubber, waterproof, insulated boots are hot and too heavy generally for summer hiking. They have a tendency to make the feet perspire, as does all fully waterproof and unventilated footwear. Nevertheless, they are excellent for cold weather hiking.

The Barker or Sno-Pak Boot. This is a versatile boot for wet weather hiking. Many guides of Alaska, Canada, and our own Pacific Northwest use them and I have worn them for many years on water and snow survey treks in the Sierra Nevada and Olympic Ranges. They can be used successfully with snowshoes. (Hard-heeled

A type of shoepak.

boots will generally damage the webbing of snowshoes if they are worn very often.) They do not, however, give much support to one's ankles and are a poor substitute for ski boots. Many outfitters supply them especially L. L. Bean, Inc., (See the Appendix for names and addresses of outfitters.)

Sneakers Have Their Uses on the Trail

Many outdoor writers and sportsmen frown on the use of sneakers (tennis shoes) in the backwoods. Over the years, however, I have noticed thousands of hikers during the summer months along the Appalachian Trail, the Northwoods, Rocky Mountains, and even members of the famous Sierra Club along the high, rough Sierra Nevada Range of California who were shod with this type of footwear. Heavy-soled ankle-high tennis shoes work well for short hiking jaunts; however, they are not helpful for the person with weak ankles. Nor will they last very long on a rocky trail. The best type of sneaker is the leather top basketball shoe. They are economical, lightweight, and sure-footed and will outlast the regular tennis type shoe. I usually take a pair along on trips and wear them in camp while airing or drying out my hiking boots. They also make excellent walkout shoes in case your boots become damaged beyond camp repair — it does happen occasionally.

Nevertheless, they do have their drawbacks. they wet through easily, they cause excessive perspiration to accumulate, and they let your socks and feet become dirty along dusty trails, but their inexpensiveness and other good points outweigh these inconveniences.

Boot Care

Most people take good care of their cars, boats, and other outdoor equipment, but they seem to slip up on the care of their hiking boots. Here are a few pointers to make your footwear last years longer; this goes for other leather goods too!

- Don't dry your boots in extreme heat — near the furnace, oven, fireplace, steam pipes, too close to your campfire, or even in the hot sun.
- When you are through using your boots or shoes, brush them and then wipe them off with a damp cloth.
- Boot grease should be applied at least once a week while out on the trail, and just before storing them for the season.
- If the leather is dry, a good application of saddle soap will clean and soften.
- Only special ski-boot grease or wax should be applied to this type of boot.
- Neat's-foot oil will soften leather and keep it more or less water repellent. Boot grease will add to this repellency.
- Pecard and other brand names of grease are excellent. Take a small can along in your knapsack.

8

Land Navigation — How the Hiker Can Stay Oriented

Pathfinding with Maps

A MAP MOST commonly refers to representation of the surface of the earth or a section of it — a drawn picture of the land as seen from above. To the outdoorsman, maps are the street signs of the wilderness. Therefore, reading a map correctly, requires some thought and study. You must know how to interpret and understand the map and its symbols and you must develop the ability to visualize the land from the map, and the map from the land. Nothing in land navigation is more important!

Being able to read and understand a topographical contour map can be fun for the whole family. If you can understand and follow a simple automobile road map, you need only a little close observation in order to be able to do the same with a geographical survey contour map.

Map Subdivisions from Public Land Surveys

As soon as you become familiar with the rectangular subdivisions formed through public land surveys, you can find any particular parcel of land anywhere in the country just as simply as you now find city blocks and buildings through the use of street names and numbers. You will note vertical and horizontal lines on your geological survey map. These, or at least a good number of them, mark the various subdivisions established by law for public lands. Not all of the lines described below will appear on all maps, for obviously a large-scale map will not cover enough area to show some of the larger divisions, and conversely, a small-scale map covering a bigger area will not contain the small divisions. However, it is useful to know what the markings mean. (Blank white areas on some maps indicate unsurveyed regions.)

Division Into 24-Mile Tracts. Surveyors first establish an initial point, by astronomical observations. A *principal meridian,* conforming to a true meridian of longitude, is established through the initial point and extending north and south. A *base line,* conforming to a true parallel of latitude, is also established through the initial point and extending east and west. *Standard parallels* are then established, conforming to true parallels of latitude, at 24-mile intervals along the principal meridian and running both east and west from it. *Guide meridians,* conforming to true meridians of longitude, run from 24-mile points established on the base line and standard parallels and extend north until they intersect the next standard parallel or base line. You will note that these tracts are not perfect 24-mile-square rectangles but, because of the curvature of the

Land division into 24-mile tracts.

earth's surface, measure slightly less than 24 miles on their northern boundary.

Division Into 6-Mile-Square Townships. The larger tracts are divided into townships, each 6-miles square, by the establishment of meridianal lines known as *range lines* and latitudinal lines called *township lines.* Range lines run north from points established at 6-mile intervals on the base line and standard parallels until they intersect the next standard parallel or base line. They are numbered east and west from the principal meridian. Township lines join the township corners already established at 6-mile intervals on the principal meridian,

2nd. Standard Parallel North

etc. | 4 West | 3 West | 2 West | 1 West | 1 East | 2 East | 3 East | 4 East | 5 East | etc. |

Range | Range | Range | Range | Range | Range | Range | Range | Range

T7N R11E

etc.

1st Standard Parallel North

Standard Township Corners

Township 5 North

Closing Township Corners

Township 4 North

Meridian West

T2N R4W

Meridian

T3N R3E

Meridian

Township 3 North

Township 2 North

Meridian East

Meridian East

Base

Principal Meridian

Initial Point Line

Meridian

Township 1 North

1st. Guide

T2S R3W

1st. Guide

6 Miles less conv. in genl. 1862

2nd Guide

Township 1 South

Township 2 South

3rd Guide

T3S R7E

etc.

1st. Standard Parallel South

6 Miles

Land subdivision into townships.

guide meridians, and range lines. They are numbered north and south from the base line.

Section Lines. Townships are next divided into sections, each of which is as nearly 1 mile square as possible. These subdivisions are made by latitudinal and longitudinal lines established at intervals of 1 mile, thus forming 36 sections to the township. When convergence of the lines prevents the establishment of 36 regular mile-square sections, the extra large or small sections are thrown to the north and west sides of the township. On some sections of a map it will be noted that certain townships are only 5½ sections wide, and that some

FOREST SERVICE LOCATION POSTER
T. 6S   R. 2IE

6	5	4	3	2	1
7	8	9	10	11	12
18	17	16	15	14	13
19	20	21	22	23	24
30	29	28	27	26	25
31	32	33	34	35	36

POINT INDICATED BY TACK IS
__O_ CHS __O_ OF __O_ CORNER

FORM 488

W.K.M. 8 1968 S. P. N. S.

Survey or timber markers showing township plat.

sections in townships are not square. This happens when old survey lines do not join up properly with newer ones.

Sections are numbered beginning with No. 1, which is at the *northeast* corner of the township. The series proceeds *westward* to the northwest corner of the township, where section No. 6 is found. No. 7 is immediately *south* of this, and the series then proceeds *eastward* to No. 12, which is south of No. 1 and back and forth, as shown in the illustration, until No. 36 is reached in

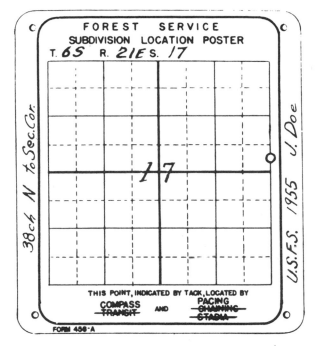

Location poster for indicating section lines of the type used at a round or trail crossing of a section line.

the southeast bottom corner of the township.

Section Subdivisions. A system of subdivisions has been devised whereby tracts of land less than a section may be described. Each boundary line of a section is marked at the center with a "quarter" corner, and a line from such corner to the one directly opposite divides a section into halves. It is divided into quarters by connecting the corners on the other sides. Note the illustrations.

Land Descriptions

It is important that hikers and other outdoorsmen familiarize themselves with methods used in describing lands. The first information given in general land description is the exact description of a section or its subdivisions. Next comes the township number, north or south of a base line, followed by the range number, east or west of a meridian. Sometimes the name or number of the principal meridian or base line is also given.

Thus several sections might be described as: Sections 1, 2, 3, and 4 (or Sections 1–4, inclusive, Township 10 South, Range 1 East of a certain meridian or base line. The abbreviated form of the above description would be: Secs. 1–4, T.10 S. R. 1 E., etc.

A *half-section* might be described as: E ½ Sec. 2, T. 16 N., R. 10 W., etc.

A *quarter-section* would be: NE ¼ Sec. 20, T. 5 N., R. 8 W., etc.

A *quarter-quarter section* would be: SE ¼ NE ¼ Sec. 2, T. 5 N., R. 10 E.

Here are the most important area divisions useful for map reference:

Acre: An area containing 43,560 square feet of land. It is equivalent to 10 square chains (One chain is 66 feet long).

Section: The section is an area of 1-mile-square, containing 640 acres.

Township: An area 6 miles wide by 6 miles long; its total area is 36 square miles.

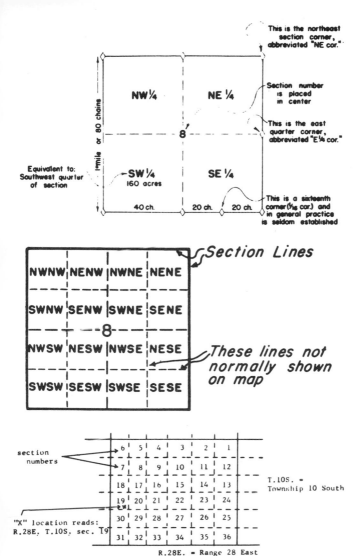

Top: Subdivision of section into quarter sections.
Middle: Subdivision of quarter sections.
Bottom: How to locate on your topographic or
United States Forest Service map.

Map Scale

Map scale may be shown by a statement of how many miles are represented by an inch on the map — 2 inches to the mile, 1 inch to the mile, ½ or ¼ inch to the mile. Trail travelers and other outdoorsmen, should look for large-scale maps. Small scale doesn't give enough clear detail.

Another map scale in use is a line divided into intervals and marked to indicate what the units or intervals represent on the ground. This is known as a graphic scale.

STANDARD SCALES AND PRICES OF THE NATIONAL TOPOGRAPHIC MAP SERIES

SERIES

7.5 minute	1:24,000
15 minute	1:62,500
1:63,360 (Alaska)	1:63,360
30 minute	1:125,000
1:250,000	1:250,000
1:1,000,000	1:1,000,000

SCALE	PRICE
1 inch equals 2,000 feet	$0.50
1 inch equals about one mile	.50
1 inch equals one mile	.50
1 inch equals about two miles	.50
1 inch equals about four miles	.75
1 inch equals about sixteen miles	1.00

A map scale may also be represented by a fraction, such as 1:24,000. This merely means that every unit of measurement on the map is represented by 24,000 similar units on the earth's surface. The representative fraction method is used on all topographic maps of this country. A conversion table of most frequent ones in use is shown in the illustration.

What Your Topographic Map Will Show

The symbols on your Geological Survey topographical contour map will indicate the date the map was printed, its scale and declination for that particular map area. It will also indicate the following: sections, townships, ranges, contour elevations, roads, trails, streams, rivers, lakes, peaks and other pertinent information. With this information plus a little experience in the woods and in camping, you should not have any fear of traveling through strange terrain. By orienting your map with the land, you can reach any place shown on the map.

What Declination Means

Declination is a term used by land surveyors and outdoorsmen; variation, meaning the same thing, is a term used by marine navigators. The terms mean the angle between true north and magnetic north. Most Geological Survey maps show a compass rose or arrow pointing to true north, with a half arrow pointing to magnetic north.

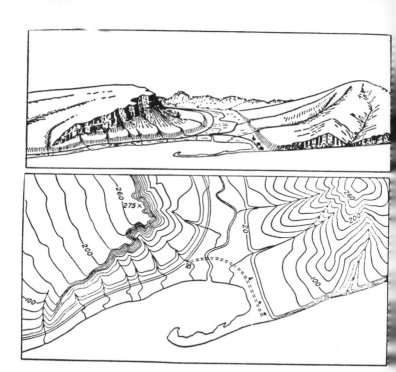

A. A landscape in perspective and the same landscape in contour lines. Note especially that lines are far apart for level land, almost touch for cliffs.

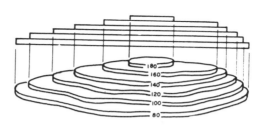

B. Contour lines show elevation above sea level.

CONTOURS SHOW LAND SHAPES & ELEVATION

The shape of the land, portrayed by contours, is the distinctive characteristic of topographic maps.

Contours are imaginary lines following the ground surface at a constant elevation above sea level.

The contour interval is the regular elevation difference separating adjacent contour lines on maps.

Contour intervals depend on ground slope and map scale; they vary from 5 to 200 feet. Small contour intervals are used for flat terrain; larger intervals for rugged mountain areas.

Supplementary dashed or dotted contours, at less than the regular interval, are used in flat areas.

Index contours, every fourth or fifth line, are heavier than others, and have elevation figures.

Hachures, form lines, and symbol patterns are also used to show some kinds of topographic forms.

Relief shading, an overprint giving a three-dimensional effect, is used on some quadrangle maps.

Backpack hiker orients himself on his map and lays out a compass course to the point he wants to reach. He then takes a compass bearing on the point he wants to reach and is ready to take off.

How to Orient a Map

In order to use a map as a means of identifying places in an area, it first must be oriented with the terrain. This can be accomplished quickly if you have a compass with you. You can orient both map and compass to compensate for magnetic declination very easily. Lay the map on a level spot on the ground, or on a stump or a rock, and place the compass on it. If you know your exact whereabouts and can find it on the map, place the compass on this point, Next, line up north and south on the compass with the north and south cardinal lines (or grid lines) on the map. Turn the map and compass until the needle parallels the line of magnetic declination shown as a half arrow either at the bottom of the map or in the upper right hand corner. Both your compass and map are now oriented for that area.

Stated more simply: place the compass on the map with the compass sighting line pointing to the north on the map. The map is then turned until the needle reads north. The directions on the map now coincide with the directions on the surface of the earth and the map is said to be oriented.

Orienting a Map Without a Compass. You can orient a map without a compass by rotating the map until the direction of a line drawn from any point to any other point on the map will be same as that between those two points on the ground.

Another method requires that the observer's position on the map be known as closely as possible, and that one point shown on the map be identifiable on the land. Imagine a line drawn between the observer's position on the map and the position of the identified point on

Hard surface, heavy duty road, four or more lanes ....

Hard surface, heavy duty road, two or three lanes ....

Hard surface, medium duty road, four or more lanes ....

Hard surface, medium duty road, two or three lanes ....

Improved light duty road ....

Unimproved dirt road—Trail ....

Dual highway, dividing strip 25 feet or less ....

Dual highway, dividing strip exceeding 25 feet ....

Road under construction ....

Railroad: single track—multiple track ....

Railroads in juxtaposition ....

Narrow gage: single track—multiple track ....

Railroad in street—Carline ....

Bridge: road—railroad ....

Drawbridge: road—railroad ....

Footbridge ....

Tunnel: road—railroad ....

Overpass—Underpass ....

Important small masonry or earth dam ....

Dam with lock ....

Dam with road ....

Canal with lock ....

Buildings (dwelling, place of employment, etc.) ....

School—Church—Cemeteries ....

Buildings (barn, warehouse, etc.) ....

Power transmission line ....

*Topographic map symbols (variations will be found
on older maps).*

Telephone line, pipeline, etc. (labeled as to type) .... _ _ _ _ _ _ _ .

Wells other than water (labeled as to type) .... o Oil .... o Gas

Tanks; oil, water, etc. (labeled as to type) .... • • ● ⊘ Water

Located or landmark object—Windmill .... o .... ✗

Open pit, mine, or quarry—Prospect .... ⚒ x

Shaft—Tunnel entrance .... ▪ .... Y

Horizontal and vertical control station:

    tablet, spirit level elevation .... BM △ 3899

    other recoverable mark, spirit level elevation .... △ 3938

Horizontal control station: tablet, vertical angle elevation .... VABM △ 2914

    any recoverable mark, vertical angle or checked elevation .... △ *5675*

Vertical control station: tablet, spirit level elevation .... BM ✗ 945

    other recoverable mark, spirit level elevation .... ✗ 890

Checked spot elevation .... *✗5923*

Unchecked spot elevation—Water elevation .... ✗ *5657* *870*

Boundary: national .... **▬ ▬ ▬ ▬**

    state .... **▬ ▬ ▬**

    county, parish, municipio .... **▬ ▬ ▬**

    civil township, precinct, town, barrio .... **▬ ▬ ▬ ▬**

    incorporated city, village, town, hamlet .... -▬--▬- -▬--

    reservation, national or state .... **▬ · ▬ ·**

    small park, cemetery, airport, etc. .... --------------

    land grant .... **▬ ·· ▬ ··**

Township or range line, U.S. land survey .... ▬▬▬▬

Township or range line, approximate location .... ▬ ▬ ▬ ▬ ·

Section line, U.S. land survey .... ▬▬▬▬

Section line, approximate location .... ▬ ▬ ▬ ▬ ·

Township line, not U.S. land survey .... ·············

Section line, not U.S. land survey .... ···········

Section corner: found—indicated	+ +
Boundary monument: land grant—other	▫ ▫
U.S. mineral or location monument	▲

Index contour		Intermediate contour	
Supplementary contour		Depression contours	
Fill		Cut	
Levee		Levee with road	
Mine dump		Wash	
Tailings		Tailings pond	
Strip mine		Distorted or broken surface	
Sand area		Gravel beach	

Perennial streams		Intermittent streams	
Elevated aqueduct		Aqueduct tunnel	
Water well—Spring		Disappearing stream	
Small rapids		Small falls	
Large rapids		Large falls	
Intermittent lake		Dry lake	
Foreshore flat		Rock or coral reef	
Sounding—Depth curve	10	Piling or dolphin	o
Exposed wreck		Sunken wreck	
Rock, bare or awash—dangerous to navigation			

Marsh (swamp)		Submerged marsh	
Wooded marsh		Mangrove	
Woods or brushwood		Orchard	
Vineyard		Scrub	
Inundation area		House omission area	

Colors distinguish classes of map features

BLACK — for roads, buildings, names and boundaries.

BLUE — for water features, lakes, rivers and glaciers.

BROWN — for relief or land features portrayed by contour lines.

GREEN — for weeded cover, forest, brush and orchards.

RED — to emphasize important roads, land sub-divisions.

LOG					
STEP NO.	DISTANCE IN YDS	FORWARD AZIMUTH MAG	GRID DECLINATION CORRECTION	GRID AZIMUTH	NOTES
1	750	12°	3°	15°	
2	865	27°	3°	30°	
3	1000	52°	3°	55°	NW TIP OF X LAKE
4	600	62°	3°	65°	

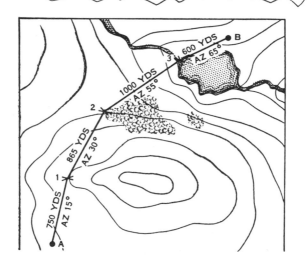

Dead reckoning log and notations.

the land. Turn the map around until this line, if extended, passes through the point on the land. The map is then oriented.

How to Ascertain Your Exact Location

There are times when you will want to know your exact location and distance from a certain point on the land.

Locating your exact position on a map is possible when two known landmarks indicated on the map can be seen from your position. Take a bearing by sighting your compass on the landmark. Then transpose this bearing line on your oriented map by drawing a line between your position on through the landmark. Repeat the procedure with the second landmark. You are now located at the intersection of these bearing lines.

You can measure the distance from point to point by using the scale on your map. However, this will be airline distance and does not allow for up and down slopes or the winding of the path.

Land Navigation by Dead Reckoning

Dead reckoning means finding your location by continuous plotting of where you have been. It is accomplished by recording and plotting a series of compass courses, each measured both as to distance and direction from a known starting point, in order to provide a plot from which the navigator's location can be determined. The most important item in navigating by dead reckoning is keeping an accurate log! Note the example in the illustration.

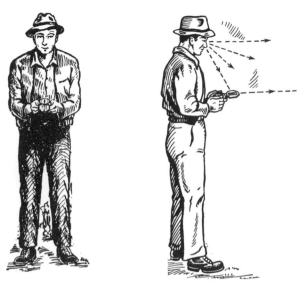

Hold the compass in both hands with your elbows firmly against your sides and with your weight evenly distributed on both feet. Prolonging the line of sight. Look along the sighting line and then raise your eyes to prolong the line of sight ahead. Do not move your head; raise your eyes.

Compass Fundamentals

There are a number of good compasses on the market. Several of the better known models are shown in the illustrations. Be sure to read the instructions that come with your compass and be sure you understand them. However, all a compass will do *for you* on a backpacking trip is indicate magnetic north (or true north if the compass has been adjusted for declination for the particular area it is being used in), allow you to orient your map quickly, to take compass bearings, and to check backsights, (reverse compass bearings). Having a compass with you will not prevent you from becoming lost if you are not observant; you must know how to take bearings and backsights.

An azimuth compass is the easier to operate for the average hikes. It is one on which the face of a fixed or floating dial is graduated into 360 degrees. The circle formed by its face is called an "azimuth circle." Numbering of the circle begins with zero (0°) which is north and proceeds *clockwise;* 90° is east, 180° is south, 270° is west, and 360°, the same as zero, is north. The 360 degrees of your compass dial are 360 different paths you may follow.

Determining an Azimuth

This is a simple operation with a magnetic azimuth compass:

- To an object on the land: To determine the azimuth of an object, tree, peak, etc., align the rear sight and front sight of the compass with the object. The number under the stationary compass index is the desired magnetic azimuth.

- To a point you have picked out on a map: Draw a line on the map connecting your position and the point you want to travel to. Orient the map by matching it with the surrounding terrain — or you can do it by aligning the magnetic North line on the map with the magnetic North of your particular location, as indicated by your com-

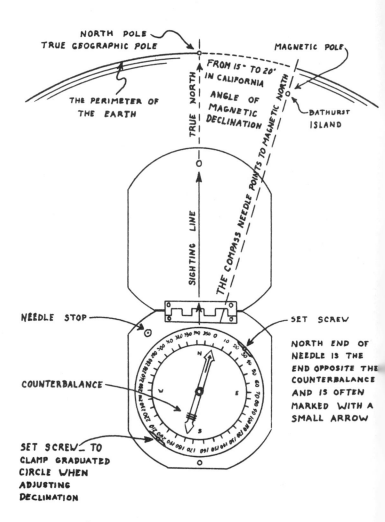

NORTH POLE
TRUE GEOGRAPHIC POLE

MAGNETIC POLE

FROM 15° TO 20°
IN CALIFORNIA

ANGLE OF
MAGNETIC
DECLINATION

TRUE NORTH

THE COMPASS NEEDLE POINTS TO MAGNETIC NORTH

THE PERIMETER OF
THE EARTH

BATHURST
ISLAND

SIGHTING LINE

NEEDLE STOP

SET SCREW

COUNTERBALANCE

NORTH END OF
NEEDLE IS THE
END OPPOSITE THE
COUNTERBALANCE
AND IS OFTEN
MARKED WITH A
SMALL ARROW

SET SCREW TO
CLAMP GRADUATED
CIRCLE WHEN
ADJUSTING
DECLINATION

*The United States Forest Service compass, typical
of those which can be adjusted to get true readings.*

The Leupold Sportsman compass.

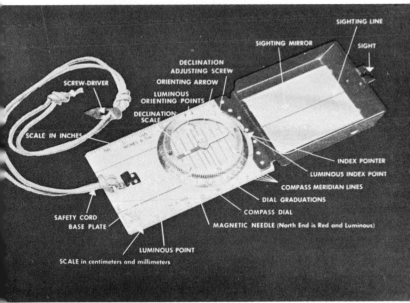

The Silva Ranger compass.

pass. Next, place the compass on the map so that the compass direction line points toward the point you wish to travel to and with hair or sighting-line directly along the line drawn on the map. The stationary index reading now indicates the magnetic azimuth of the point on the map.

Rule for Obtaining Back Azimuth Reading. You should check your back course (azimuth) once in awhile to make sure that you haven't strayed from your primary course or bearing. Example:

- When your compass bearing is 180° or less, *add* 180 degrees to obtain a back azimuth. Example: If your primary course or bearing is 60°, *add* 180°. Your back azimuth will then be 240° (60° + 180° = 240°).

- When your compass bearing is more than 180°, *subtract* 180 degrees. Example: If your primary course is 310°, you should *subtract* 180°. The back azimuth for this particular reading will then be 130° (310° − 180° = 130°).

9

Hiking with Backpack and Burro

Hiking with Burros

THE LEAST EXPENSIVE way to enter the wilderness mountain regions without having to tote your outfit on your back is the hiking pack trip. In this manner, a pack animal ambles along carrying the load, led by the unburdened hiker. By using a "reluctant" burro, horse, or mule, the hiker can take along more equipment and wet-pack canned goods and can travel further and stay longer than when he carried it all on his back. The length of the jaunt can be even further extended if the hiker will also carry a light pack, or he can take along an extra pack animal to carry the added supplies.

Children Can Ride

Another reason to consider pack animals is that small children can rest their legs by riding occasionally, and therefore they make more headway than when they are just hiking. A small child riding on his father's back or on top of a burro can, as a rule, ride happily and in comfort for about an hour or two; after that he needs a break. An older child can ride on the back of a burro packed with saddle and a kyack, but the top pack should be omitted. Some type of pad should be placed between the child and the pack ropes to prevent chafing. At the age of 5, 6, or 7, the youngster can ride along on the back of a donkey. Beyond 8 years of age children can walk much of the time, even when packing a child's size knapsack loaded with a few of his personal belongings. However, it is wise to have a riding burro along so that a child may rest his legs from time to time. The mother or other children can rest their backs once in a while by attaching their packs to the burro's saddle when no one else is riding it. If knapsacks are hung from the riding saddle, be careful that the packs do not swing back and forth and chafe the animal's hide.

Why Burros Are Favored

I mention burros because they are used more for this type of trek than are horses and mules. The last two animals mentioned travel a little too fast for the average hiker and are apt to step on the hiker's heels (and toes, too, at times) when led.

Horses and mules must be shod, while the tough little donkey goes barefooted. With the larger animals, shoeing can create quite a problem in the field. An animal who looses a shoe along the trail and is not reshod shortly afterwards will either become lame or else will damage the hoof edges to a degree that he will need weeks to recover. So the backpacker who isn't experienced in shoeing a horse or a mule will have to interrupt his journey and wait until a packer or patrolling Ranger comes along to his assistance.

Anyone handling stock should know how to treat a sick, lame, or injured animal in the field. Sores and wounds should be treated and kept as clean and sterile as possible. Don't ever forget that animals are warm-blooded too and that they have feelings. A snakebitten animal should be treated the same as a person (see First Aid chapter).

Cost of Rental Stock

Burros generally rent at $3.50 per day; horses and mules run $7.50 to $8 per day. Rates may vary from year to year. All pack station operators are required to have a Special Use Permit in the National Parks and Forests.

Many pack stations will refuse to rent horses or mules unless a packer goes along. In Canada and in some states, a guide is required by law. You can easily understand why some owners require an experienced packer to go along with these larger animals. They have too much invested in their pack station and stock and too short a season to take risks. They have seen too many of their pack animals returned lame, galled, sore-backed, and sometimes half-starved after a trip where the renter tied them up at night and never let them loose to graze, or neglected to carry grain along to feed these hard working creatures. Or, alerted by one of these tenderfoot's animals returning to the home corral, hobbles and all, they have lost time and money when they have had to head out and rescue these dudes, who were stranded through their own carelessness or inexperience.

How You Can Learn to Pack an Animal

One way to avoid errors is to read up on the subject. Gain the book knowledge — then go out into the field and practice. Another way is to go to the nearest pack station and have the packer or a guide teach you the rudiments. For recommended reading see the Bibliography.

Generally, it is best to buy one or more of these fine "how-to" books and take them home where you can relax, read, and study them at your leisure. Those not wishing to purchase them may obtain the books at their local library. If they are not available there, the librarian can request them from the main library at the state capital.

The Planning Phase

The planning of a hike-in with pack stock is almost as much fun for the family or a group of friends as the actual trip on the trail. There is much work entailed in preparing for a jaunt of this magnitude, but it is all enjoyable and interesting. Maps must be obtained and studied and proposed routes outlined. It must be decided whether to return the same way or make a loop trip out of it, since the pack stock must be returned to the point of departure. If you end your jaunt otherwise, the animals will have to be either led, ridden, or trucked back by someone to their home corral. This can turn out to be rather expensive.

Distance to be traveled must be taken into consideration and time schedules worked out. Menus must be planned that are satisfactory to all participants; the food and gear check lists must be gone over to insure that nothing has been left to chance. The availability of pack stock will determine your jump-off time. Burros or other stock must be reserved several months in advance, since most pack stations are booked full during the summer vacation period and fall hunting season.

Determining the Number of Burros Needed

To determine the number of "donks" needed, the approximate load weight must be calculated. To do this, I weigh all items. I personally use a spring scale that will weigh loads up to 50 pounds. You can also use a bathroom scale for heavy loads (weigh yourself, then weigh yourself with the load and subtract). For loads up to 10 pounds I use my wife's small post-office-type kitchen scale that is graduated in ounces. This small scale is useful when I am weighing food and small items for a straight backpack jaunt.

The number of pounds of food that must be provided can be determined before actual purchase is made. If the menu will be that of the backpacker, 2¼ pounds per man per day is a reliable figure. I find that 2½ to 2¾ pounds is a better estimate for the group of heavy eaters

PACK OUTFIT EQUIPMENT CHECKLIST

Personal Gear
  Toilet kit
  Hunting and fishing license
  Compass and maps
  Wash cloths and towels
Clothing — Inner
  Lightweight wool shirt
  Heavyweight wool shirt
  Medium weight wool pants
  Wool underwear (2)
  Socks, 6 pr., wool
  Bandanna handkerchiefs
Clothing — Outer
  Saddle slicker
  Hunting cap with ear flaps
  Red hunting hat with brim
  Down jacket
  Wool cruiser coat
  Mountain climbing boots
  Barker (or Sno-Paks) boots
  Rain parka and pants
  Leather work gloves
  Wool mittens
  Suspenders
  Camp moccasins
Miscellaneous
  Sun glasses (yellow lens)
  Binoculars
  Spotting scope, small tripod
  Extra inner-soles
  Extra bulbs and batteries
  Flashlight
  Pocket knife (BSA model)
  Sheath knife (3½-inch blade)
  Battery-powered shaver
  Hot-water bag or bottle
  Thermos bottle (qt. size)
  Sharpening stone
  Boot waterproofing
  First-aid kit
  Personal medicines
  Smoking gear and tobacco
  Pocket warmer
  Flannel pajamas
  Hooded sweatshirt and pants
  Air mattress
  Down sleeping bag
  Bed roll
  Air pump
  Camera, extra film, and gear
  Duffel bags
  Saddle bags
  Snake bite kit
  Waterproof match safe

  Waterproofed matches
Firearms Gear
  Rifle, scope-sighted
  Rifle, iron sights or
    Shotgun (if bird hunting)
  Hooded leather scabbard
  Cleaning kit, firearms
  Ammunition
  Scope hoods
Camp Gear
  Light canvas fly, 12 x 12 ft.
  Tarpaulin, canvas, 10 x 10 ft.
  Coleman lantern
  Axe, single-bit 3 lbs. head
  Camp saw, folding
  White gas, square 5 gal. can
  Strainer
  Extra generators and mantles
    for lantern
  Shovel, forester type 3 lbs.
  50 ft. ½-inch rope
  Ball twine
  Toilet tissue
  Pliers, lineman type
  Aluminum grill
  Wire grill
  Reflector oven
  Pressure cooker (optional)
    Cooking pans
  Kettles
  Kitchen gear, knives, forks,
    spoons, pancake turner, etc.
  Tableware
  Bottle and can-opener
  Aluminum foil
  Lunch gear, wax paper, sacks
  Salt and pepper shakers
  Soap and dish towels, detergents
  Kitchen Maid, S.O.S. pads
  Pot holders
  Paper towels
  Large cooking fork
  Dutch oven
  Large iron fry pan
  Nesting cook kit
  Coffee pot
  Dish pan
  Wash pan
  Oil cloth
  Plates
  Cups
  Butcher knife
  Paring knife
  Insect repellent

I travel with. Also, we often feed some hungry wayfarer along the trail who has run short of supplies or who stops by to visit our camp.

Additional weight means extra animals to pack it. Several guide books mention 100-pound loads for burros and up to 200-pounds for horses and mules. Grass-fed animals can pack this size load, but they can't do it day in and day out and keep in shape all summer. Standard weight load for burros is 50 to 75 pounds, depending on size, age, and state of the animal's health. Recommended weight for horses and mules is 150 to 185 pounds. Most pack station owners do not want their stock loaded beyond the above-mentioned weights.

Information The Packer Must Have

The packer will want to know well in advance what date you want to leave; where you plan on going; how many in your party; how long you will be gone, and the date you expect to return. He will also need to know the approximate total weight to be packed so that the number of animals can be determined. A deposit must be sent in advance to secure the reservation.

How to Contact a Pack Station Concessioner

Write to the Park Superintendent or the Forest Supervisor of the area in which you are interested and ask for a list of concessioners who rent burros and other pack stock (you sometimes have to settle for a mule). You can also write to your state Chamber of Commerce for the above information.

The Dunnage Pack-In

If you do not wish to be bothered with packing and care of animals, but do not want to pack your outfit on your back, consider the dunnage pack. You can be packed in by a professional packer to a predetermined destination, usually to a scenic lake or alpine meadow and your outfit left while you hike to your camp location. The cost is $8 per mule load, plus $25 and up per day for the packer. You pay for the day he packs your gear in and for the day he packs your outfit out. Establishing a base camp in this manner one can use it as long as the grub holds out. All kinds of side trips can be taken from this point.

If the packer is at your camp during mealtime or is required to stay over night at your camp because of the distance back to the pack station, it is up to you to feed him. So be sure that you have planned for a few extra meals in case you have a guest in camp! Also, a storm might delay your return. A sample pack outfit checklist is illustrated.

Before You Leave the Pack Station

Don't start out until you check important details. Have the packer advise you on the handling, care, and feeding of your rented burros, and ask if you should picket them or turn them loose each night to graze.

Have him show you how to pack an animal from bare-back to full pack and have him teach you to throw a simple hitch like the one-man diamond or lone ranger, as shown in the illustrations.

Equipment. The pack station will furnish all the necessary pack equipment, nevertheless, it is well to know what this includes so that you can check and be sure that it is all there and that it is in good condition or properly repaired. The packer will replace any faulty equipment if you bring it to his attention. Each pack animal should have a halter, lead rope (preferably one with a snap-swivel at one end), a pack saddle and saddle blanket or pad — free of pine needles and other abrasive material and as clean as possible — two fitted kyacks, a mantle (canvas pack cover) and at least a 30-foot pack rope. Don't forget to take along a curry comb and brush to keep the animals' backs brushed free of all debris and dirt (pack animals are apt to roll in the dirt or dust after being unloaded).

Ask if hobbles will be necessary. If you are to picket the burros each night, be sure to take picket-pins along that have a free-working swivel at the top so that the animals will not get wound up short in the picket-rope. Take a grazing bell or two along if you are to turn the animals loose to graze. Ask the packer if your animals have any particular faults such as kicking or biting. Generally, burros are not hobbled. If you picket one animal, usually his companions will stick around close by. Hearing their grazing bells near camp is a wonderful sound when you awaken in the morning, for you know that you won't have to hike a long distance looking for the beast.

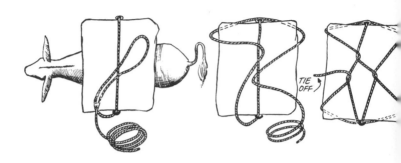

The one-man or government diamond hitch.

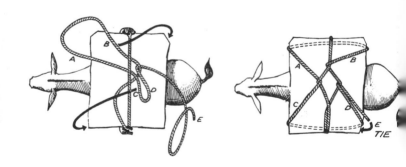

The lone ranger hitch.

Halters must be snug fitting, otherwise a smart burro may slip his head out and perhaps head for the home corral. Good blankets are essential to sound backs. *Don't* accept any matted that are hard with sweat and grime or ones full of holes. A double-rigged pack saddle is generally best for travel on steep trails. Some packers only use single-rigged outfits. On a double-rigged pack saddle there are two cinches. The front cinch is pulled up tight, but not so snug that you can't get at least two fingers between the cinch and the animal's chest. The forward cinch should be at least 3 inches back of the front shoulder so that the flesh will not be wrinkled causing a hard-to-heal sore. The rear cinch hangs more or less loose so that the animal can breathe without distress. The breast-strap keeps the load from moving backward.

The part of the harness that goes over the animal's rear is called the breech. This keeps the pack saddle and load from slipping forward when you are descending a steep trail grade. Some animals are touchy when the breeching is pulled down over their rear and their tails pulled free over the outside of the harness — so be careful that you don't get kicked. If you will stand a short distance away with one arm rather straight out and one hand on the beast's rump you can drop the gear over the rear and handle the operation without danger. If you can't free the tail without the animal making a fuss, just leave it; often he will free his tail somewhere along the trail when he wants to switch a bothersome fly.

Kyacks and Panniers. Kyacks and panniers are con-

During a trail ride halt, a packer completes a double diamond hitch.

Burro carrying box-kyack.

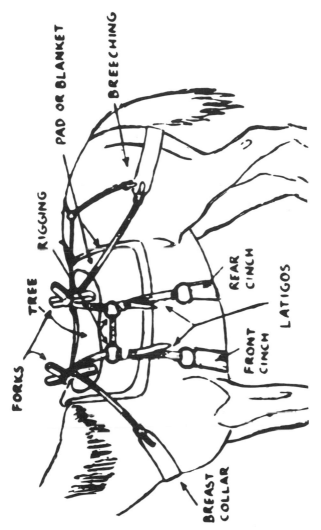

The pack saddle — proper position and parts.

tainers that hang from each side of the pack saddle and are made of either canvas or leather. If they are made of plywood, they are called box-kyacks. The box-type kyacks are just large enough to carry two 5-gallon kerosene cans standing side by side. I prefer this type of kyack. Packed properly, it offers less breakage of fragile gear than the flexible kind. If you cut the top out of a new 5-gallon can, it can be slipped inside the box kyack and the gear and equipment or foodstuff can be packed inside. Later at camp, it will make an excellent water bucket if a wire bail is attached for a handle.

The kyacks are suspended from the cross-tree or sawbuck pack saddle by leather loops that are adjustable, to allow the panniers or kyacks to ride level. Canvas slings are used instead of kyacks when there is bulky or odd shaped gear to be packed. If you use these, be sure to have the packer show you how to pack them; they are not as easy to handle as kyacks are.

The pack rope should be at least 30 feet long. I prefer to use a braided cotton rope, as they are soft to handle when dry. A 3- or 4-twist manila rope is stronger and more durable but rougher on the hands. A pair of soft leather gloves comes in handy when you pack.

How Fast and How Far in a Day?

With pack stock you will average between 8 and 10 miles a day; don't count on over 12 any day, although it can be done with a light load and an early start. To enjoy a burro pack trip, plan short hauls the first few days, and allow time for layover days at the most scenic camps, where you can bathe, rest, fish, take pictures, or just loaf.

Hitting the Desert Trails

The Western Deserts

There are more than 10 million square miles of deserts in the world. A considerable amount of the over 400 million acres of public land in our country is classified as "desert." The three deserts in the United States that interest most "desert-rat" backpackers are the Mojave, Colorado, and Sonoran located mostly in the Southwestern states.

To many people, the desert seems to be a desolate, uninhabited wasteland — a region of little beauty. But they just haven't opened their eyes to observe, or haven't taken the time or picked the right season to look.

Types of Terrain

Generally, the term "desert" is applied to those areas where plant life does not thrive, either because of cold or aridness. The cold deserts are high mountain ice fields or high plateau areas; the drought deserts can be cold and windy too in winter and extremely hot and sunny during the long summer months. Elevations and temperatures can run to the extremes within a short distance. For example, Bad Water in Death Valley is at 272 feet below sea level, and just 40 airline miles due west, Mt. Whitney rises to 14,496 feet in elevation.

The Best Time to Go

Most people come to the deserts of Arizona, Utah, Nevada, New Mexico, parts of Texas or California in April or May, when rains sweep across the parched land. Shortly thereafter, the desert blooms out—flowers cover hundreds of acres of ground, as far as the eye can see. This is the period when people drive out for the day and hike through the colorful flowers, taking snapshots or home movies, or just breathing in the dry desert air for the pleasure and health it brings.

But others prefer to drive off the main road and travel down a quiet side road to a spot that suits their fancy. There they set up a base camp near a desert spring or natural desert tank among the rocks, then backpack further out for a day or more. Many enjoy the desert resorts at Palm Springs and Death Valley in the winter months where they can hike and explore the surrounding terrain. Some enter the desert land for health reasons and slowly hike their way back to health again. Rockhounds and prospectors go out to the more remote sections at all times of the year, tramping far and wide in their search for uranium, gold, and semi-precious stones. Some go to study the flora and fauna or whatever strikes their fancy — but they do hike to points of ·vantage to do so.

Backpacking Is For All Seasons

When snow whitens trails, backpackers regretfully store their gear and hibernate from hiking and backpacking. They are prepared to wait out another long winter on last summer's memories of pleasant trail trips, or they can anticipate next summer's trek into the wilderness. But outdoorsmen have rediscovered another wilderness where they can continue their hiking and backpacking jaunts during off-season vacations or on weekends during the winter months. These off-season hikers head for the Southwest deserts, where they hike, camp, hunt and even fish — in man-made desert reservoirs or along the Colorado River that bounds Arizona and Nevada.

The Right Attitude

The reason many people haven't given the deserts of our country a thought, so far as its recreation potential is concerned, is that they picture this arid land as a trackless, lifeless, waterless wasteland of burning emptiness. No person experienced in desert lore will argue this point if you are talking about hitting the desert trails during the hot summer months. The desert does demand respect and there are dangers for those who enter this vast domain carelessly!

Winter and Summer Residents

During the winter, many of the animals hibernate. During the hot summer, in the middle of the day, the

View across Death Valley from Aquereberry Point.

Devil's Cornfield.

desert seems deserted, since most of the animals and birds are hiding from the furnace-like heat. An occasional road-runner may scurry across the sand to kill a rattlesnake hiding in the shade of a rock or bush, and you may see and pick up a friendly little horned-toad (a species of lizard), but *don't ever* attempt to pick up one of the sluggish moving Gila monsters or Mexican beaded-lizards — their bite can prove fatal. Zebra-tailed lizards as well as others you may see are not poisonous.

Toward dusk, in the cool of the evening, the desert awakens from its siesta. Desert rodents such as the antelope squirrel, kangaroo rat, and silky pocket mouse leave their burrows and seek plant and insect food, and snakes of various species, including the Western diamondback rattlers and sidewinders go hunting after rodents and other snakes and animal food. The kit fox can be heard barking in the distance, and the elf owl may add its odd voice as its eyes watch the blacktailed jack rabbit, skunk, and badger roam about through the cactus and desert bushes.

In the high plateau desert you may see deer, antelope, and desert sheep if you are very observant, or you may hear peccaries snorting as they root for food in the ground or whatever they can find (they will eat most anything).

Toward sunrise, most of the animals seek shelter to hide from the scorching heat that will arrive as the sun climbs high into the sky. This is the time to see the desert bird life. The birds head for the nearest water hole and then seek flower and plant seeds close by. The Gila woodpecker can sometimes be heard hammering away on a saguaro cactus, desert sparrows, and crystal thrashers peck for bugs in the sand, while scissor-tailed flycatchers prefer to snap them from the air. Warblers and orioles sing from their perches on desert bushes.

The Northern Sagebrush Deserts

Northern deserts offer many of the same attractions as do forested regions, but like the *southern deserts,* they contain many features that cannot be found elsewhere.

The northern sagebrush desert is characterized by scattered growths of deciduous shrubs, all of which have small leaves, usually of a silvery color. The plants are woody and sometimes resemble a miniature forest. Sagebrush forms the most important community by far.

The weather is not necessarily scorching hot, in fact some of the coldest and windiest weather in the nation occurs in these high desert areas. Both altitudes and latitudes influence the weather in an area and *the desert* is no exception. Two areas may be defined as deserts because of their low rainfall and aridness, but they may be as different as black and white because of climatic zones. Contrast, for example, the Big Bend country of Texas with certain parts of sagebrush country in Montana and Wyoming. The Texas region has a long, dry, and hot summer and appears to be desolate, the Wyoming and Montana desert sections have a shorter summer and are green and even productive. The so-called sagebrush country of south Texas differs radically from the desert portions of eastern Oregon, Washington, and California; and they in turn are far different from the weird and thrilling colored desert rock formation of Utah in the Flaming Gorge Recreation Area, or in Bryce and Zion National Parks. The saguaro-studded desert found in the Joshua Tree National Monument in southern California has another aspect when it occurs in Arizona.

*Tall saguaros and taller crags in the Coronado
National Forest, Arizona.*

The Hot and Cold of It

All deserts are hot in the summer, no doubt about that! But deserts generally cool swiftly at night. At certain times of the year desert nights can become not only cool but frigid. In the high plateau deserts, you may be perfectly comfortable in shirt sleeves and shorts as long as you are in the sun, but move around into the shade of a bluff or your tent, and even at midday you may shiver from the cold. This is especially true in the spring and fall months.

I have hunted, camped and backpacked in Montana and Wyoming sage deserts in September and I have sweated and frozen as I hiked from open stretches of sunlight to sections of shade on the off-side of a hill. And I have had the same thing happen while on patrol in the desert land of the Lake Mead National Recreation Area in Arizona and Nevada.

Proper Clothing for Desert Treks

Clothing should be planned so that you have long sleeved cotton shirts for general use. Long snag-proof pants are a *must*. A lightweight jacket and a sweater will take care of cool evenings around the campfire.

Head Gear. Never go hatless in the desert! A wide brimmed felt or straw hat is a *must!* I personally like the Ranger uniform sun helmet.

Feet and Legs. Footwear for any type of desert country must be lightweight and tough. Hikers traveling the desert trails need good rugged non-skid soles that will stick to rocks and can withstand cactus thorns and spines without puncturing. Basketball shoes or moccasins are fine around camp, but they are not practical for hiking in thorn country.

If you do a lot of hiking, protect your legs from cactus thorns by wearing a pair of regular hunter's type "briar" pants. In real brush or thorn country, I sometimes wear the "tin-pants" (canvas trousers) I used to wear when cruising timber. However, they are stiff and noisy in the brush and alarm game when hunting.

I think most desert flora and fauna will attack you unless you learn to leave it alone. An old desert-rat prospector once told me that everything in the desert either stinks, stings, or sticks. This is true to a degree — plants are pungent, desert wasps and scorpions sting, and the spines on many cacti stick if you come in contact with them.

Three Important Items You Should Pack

These three items are a pocket knife that has a long sharp thin blade, a pair of tweezers, and a small magnifying glass. These tools will come in very handy in removing the occasional cactus spines and thorns that you are bound to connect with sooner or later. Some of the hooked variety have a tendency to keep working into one's skin deeper and deeper and if not promptly removed they will cause the puncture wound to become infected and fester in a very short time.

Correct Way to Remove Cactus Spines

Never try to brush away cactus spines that get into your skin, as you are apt to break off the protruding portions making it more difficult to get hold of them with tweezers. If they break off at or below skin surface, you face a probe and dig job. Even the very tiny spines can be troublesome. First-time desert travelers often make the mistake of "feeling" these cute soft, woolly looking cactus. The fuzzy-looking "fur" is made up of thousands of exceedingly fine, tough, wiry spines — hard to dig out once they stab you. You can seldom see all of them to tweezer them out. Nevertheless, you will know that they are sticking with you until every last one is found and removed. Those that have broken off deep down where you can't get at them will fester in a few hours; and sometimes they can be squeezed out. Under these circumstances, you are taking a chance of the resulting puncture wounds turning into a bad case of infection. I have found by experience, that if you soak the injured finger or hand in quite hot, very soapy water for 15 to 20 minutes every two hours, you will usually get rid of any infection.

Need for Snakebite Kit

Desert country is snake country! So carry an emergency snakebite kit *with you* at all times. There is no danger if you use common sense. Watch where you sit, step, or walk! Keep to the open sunny spots; avoid the shady one where a "buzz-tail" may be keeping cool. Rattlesnakes and Gila monsters cannot stand heat. Generally, ten minutes in bright hot sunlight will kill a viper. Make it a point *never* to put your hands into crevices or hollows of cactus or other tree stumps, and

Cactus spines can be troublesome.

watch out when stepping off ledges or over rocks — there might be a snake on the other side. *Don't ever* wonder around carelessly at night in rattlesnake country — this is their feeding time! If you do have to move around for various reasons, put your shoes on and use a flashlight so that you can see what is in front of you. Don't become a snake casualty! A common belief is that a hair rope or any other kind of rope strung on the ground around your tent will prevent snakes from crossing it. But it just won't work! It is best to have a sewed-in floor in your tent and a door-flap that can be zippered closed to keep out crawling pests.

Tents for Desert Camping

The basics of desert knapsack camping are very different from those used when camping in woods or mountain terrain. Here you can get by with a light-weight canvas or plastic fly, however, it is best to use an insect-proof tent with a sewed-in canvas floor, with two or more screened windows and a door that can be zippered closed. This type of desert shelter will keep out the desert insects and crawling visitors such as spiders, centipedes, scorpions, unwelcome lizards, field mice and an occasional curious rattlesnake.

I recall one incident when I was stationed in the desert. A camper failed to zipper his tent opening for the night. Toward morning a spotted-skunk bit his son on the hand and shoulder as he lay asleep in his sleeping bag. Fortunately, the father had presence of mind to kill the skunk and have a laboratory test made for rabies. The test proved negative; however, it could have been otherwise. Things like this hardly ever happen, but it pays to play safe. It might be added that the tent owners gave up trying to remove the skunk musk from their tent — they finally burned it. For safety reasons, keep your tent flap tied or closed when you leave it for any length of time, and always after you retire at night!

The Jungle Hammock

Sometimes when I don't want to pack a tent, I use a jungle-hammock. With this type of tent-hammock you can sleep safely up off the ground. You are screened in with netting and the top is covered with a canvas awning or cover. These hammocks can be purchased at many surplus stores and from some outfitters for about $12 to $13.50. Or the go-light backpacker can use one of the ultra-lightweight 2- or 3-man mountain tents, but they are more expensive.

Watch Out for Wind

Most deserts are windy, at least during certain periods nearly every day. Tents not using stakes should be weighted down with gear along the inside edges, or snubbed down with rocks piled against the stays. If the tent must be staked down, tie the guylines to the center of the stakes and bury the stake horizontally in the ground about a foot deep. If the soil is very loose sand, make sure you bury the stakes *at least* a foot deep. When rocks are handy, place these on top of the buried stakes for best results. You don't want to come back to your camp sometime and find your tent blown into a cactus patch and punctured full of spine-holes.

Fuel for Your Campfire

Surprising as it may seem, fuel for a cooking or campfire is not as difficult to come by as one might think. Nevertheless, I have found it best to take along a two-burner camp stove when hiking out of a base camp that I can drive to. If I hike out from this camp over night, I sometimes take a small knapsack model. Especially if I am in a rocky fuelless area.

However, to me a cooking and campfire are cheerful and have their appeal — and they are sometimes necessary for warmth in the desert. When you can find it mesquite is one of the best desert fuels available. It burns slowly and makes a fine bed of coals. However, it is a very hard wood and needs a sharp camp saw or axe to cut it into proper firewood size. Sagebrush is oily and will burn even though green. Juniper, found in the foothills of the higher plateau deserts makes a fast hot and colorful fire. Dry cottonwood found along old dried-up stream beds will also burn hot and fast. If no wood fuel is available, gather bunches of grass and low dry plants; twist tightly together and use. Have all materials ready to cook since this type of fuel burns rapidly and lasts only a few minutes.

First Aid Along the Trail

Being Prepared

It is surprising how infrequently accidents and illnesses occur to hikers and backpackers along the woods and mountain trails. Why? Probably because most of us are apt to be more alert and careful when we know we are far from medical aid and hospital care. But it is important that all of us using the out-of-doors and remote wilderness areas be prepared to cope with any emergency situations that do come up. Through lack of care, even small cuts and scratches may become infected — and serious consequences may result.

Knowledge of First Aid

The importance of first aid to the injured cannot be overemphasized. Statistics show that the greatest number of casualties to knapsack hikers have resulted from the lack of proper emergency treatment. In some cases proper first-aid procedure may not have been followed; in others first-aid material or medicine may not have been at hand to deal with the illness or injury involved.

Accidents don't really just happen — they are caused by what people do or fail to do, or by so-called acts of God such as severe storms that bring cold or hot winds, rain, snow, and lightning — over these we have no control.

So whether you are an occasional vacationer or a continually active outdoorsman, it pays to know how to administer first aid to an injured person. Read up on the subject and take the free Standard American National Red Cross Course!

Advanced First Aid Course

The Advanced Red Cross course should be taken by ski mountaineers, rock climbers, and cross country hikers. At least one member of a group should have this advanced training and know how to cope with the more severe accidents. He should know how to clean a wound and how to close it properly by suturing it with a surgical needle and thread or with metal clamps, or, in the case of a common laceration, by closing it with a butterfly-shaped piece of adhesive tape. He should also know how to improvise and use a traction splint in case of a fractured limb. The leader of the party must know what steps he must take to properly evacuate a victim to qualified medical care.

Consulting Your Family Physician

Before anyone ventures out on a back-country back-pack jaunt of any magnitude, he should have a physical checkup. He should also be sure that he has taken care of all dental needs, so that the trip will not have to be aborted because of an aching jaw. The advanced first-aider should get advice from a doctor on what type of first-aid material and drugs he should take along and how to administer them correctly for various illnesses that might be contracted on the trek; he should also obtain prescriptions for any necessary drugs.

Immunization

Be sure that you and each member of your group have tetanus protection. Also, all members should have an innoculation against typhoid. Any member allergic to bee stings should be immunized before a trip or at least carry an anti-bee sting syringe along in case he is stung by yellowjackets or other wasps. Bee stings kill more people than poisonous vipers!

Minor Trail Injuries or Hazards

Generally poison ivy, oak, or sumac, bee stings, sunburn, foot blisters, and ankle sprains, in that order, seem to be more prevalent along the trail than other types of injuries. Bruises are next. Some hikers and backpackers move along too rapidly and are apt to slip, trip or fall — so slow down, and don't travel at night. That can be dangerous!

In the lower elevations, the hiker who wears walking shorts may acquire not only scratches or sunburned legs, but a stinging rash from nettles or poison ivy, oak, or sumac, or bee stings on his bare legs. Long pants give more protection against these hazards, and may prevent a severe viper-bite! At higher elevations, long trousers not only give some protection against the above risks, but help to prevent wind chill.

It is taken for granted that you hikers have the good judgment to familiarize themselves with the American Red Cross First Aid procedures before venturing out on a backpacking trek. In any case, here is a summary or refresher on how to treat some of minor injuries that occur.

Poison Ivy, Oak or Sumac. Consult a doctor about injecting extracts for these types of plant poisoning to produce resistance. If you have come into contact with one of these plants but blisters haven't formed yet, wash affected parts of skin thoroughly with strong soap (yellow laundry soap is best) in hottest water possible without scalding, then apply alcohol. If blisters have already formed, make a paste by heating soap and water to the consistency of lard, apply thickly to rash, allow to dry, and leave overnight. Use calamine solution from your first-aid kit if you have it.

Treatment for Bee Stings. Remove stinger. Apply ice or snow pack if available. Wet soda, ammonia, or vinegar packs will help relieve much of the pain. Follow treatment with use of cold cream or first-aid cream. Calamine lotion will relieve itching if available. If you are sensitive to bee stings, see your family doctor and arrange to take anti-bee sting shots before leaving on a jaunt.

Sunburn. To prevent sunburn use a good grade of anti-sunburn lotion, following directions. If your face and arms are already windburned or sunburned and blisters have appeared, use vaseline or zinc ointment. To prevent your eyes from becoming painfully burned, wear a good grade of sun glasses. Wear them even though it may be cloudy, especially if you are at high elevation or on water.

Blisters. When a shoulder strap, garment, or shoe chafes the skin, seek out the cause and correct it, if possible, before a blister develops (usually on the foot). The proper care of a blister is determined by its cause. If you have a friction blister for example, and the skin isn't broken, just apply a sterile band aid from your first-aid kit. (I hope you carried one.) If the blister has broken, wash carefully and dry with a sterile piece of gauze, and apply a sterile band aid. If the blister has not broken open but needs to be drained, wash with soap and water. Sterilize a needle or the point of your knife over an open flame. Puncture the blister at the edge, just enough so that you can gently press out the water or blood with a sterile pad of gauze and apply a sterile band aid or dressing as needed.

If You Sprain Your Ankle! Sprains are tears of ligaments supporting a joint. Sprains generally swell and sometimes discolor. There is tenderness, and pain when there is motion.

Apply cold compresses immediately and leave on for an hour or two. If there is a cold stream or lake nearby, soak the limb in it to reduce pain and swelling. Apply a sprained-ankle bandage, and if the injury isn't too severe, you can move about, using caution. Making use of a stick or walking staff for added balance and support can be helpful. Favor the limb as much as possible by placing most of the weight on the opposite leg. Some exercise of the affected ankle minimizes swelling and helps to promote healing, in contrast to complete rest or immobilization. Naturally, if it is a severe sprain the joint should be immobilized. A bone may even be fractured, and only an x-ray can tell for sure.

Several years ago while quail hunting near Yosemite with my friend Ranger Gallison, I slipped between two rocks and cracked my ankle. I put a sprained ankle bandage on the injury and with the aid of a 4-foot limb, I was able to hobble two miles to my car where I met up with Gallison. He drove me to the local hospital, where x-rays were taken that proved the bone was cracked. I had thought it was just a bad sprain.

Bruises. Bruises are usually discolored and tender to the touch. Treat with cold packs similar to sprain treatment. If the skin is broken, treat as an open wound.

Cuts. Cleanliness is the key to keeping minor cuts from becoming infected and complicated. Resist the urge to put a cut to your mouth or blow on it. Your mouth is full of bacteria and might cause infection. Instead, wash the cut immediately with soap and water. When the wound and surrounding skin have been cleaned, hold a sterile gauze pad over it until bleeding stops.

A mild antiseptic first-aid cream or spray may be applied, though it is not absolutely necessary. Don't use iodine, it is too harsh and can cause irritation. Finally, loosely tape on a fresh sterile pad, preferably one that is plastic coated, or if the wound is large, put on a sterile compress and bandage. Replace the dressing as often as necessary to keep the wound dry and clean.

If you are not acclimated to high elevations, take it quite easy the first few days so that you do not suffer altitude sickness which can make you feel faint, or contract a headache or nausea.

Camp Injuries

Most of the first-aid cases you will handle, if any, will be cuts and scratches from sharp-edged tools or ragged edges of food cans. The old fashioned can opener is a great tool to gouge and cut one's hands — so leave it home! Use gloves and pliers or a kettle lifter when removing hot pots or plates from the campfire during cooking. Burns can be painful, and if you are not careful, they may become infected.

If a wound is sustained by someone in the group, treat it by washing the injured part with plenty of soap and water. If the wound is small, wait until the skin around it dries, then put on an adhesive bandage. Cover a large wound with a sterile gauze pad or compress and bandage in place. If you do not have a sterile compress or pad, use a clean piece of cloth, but sterilize the part that will touch the wound by scorching it with a match or cigarette lighter flame. If the wound is infected, soak limb in hot soapy water for half an hour at least three times a day. Don't use water so hot that it will cause further irritation. For infections on the body trunk, use hot water packs.

Common Injuries, Symptoms and Treatment

On pages 194-195 is a list of injuries with indications of their symptoms and treatment (courtesy of Cutter Laboratories, Inc.) In case of injury always try to reach a doctor or nurse as soon as possible. In the meantime be calm and examine the victim carefully. Be careful not to touch wounds with your fingers. Don't move the victim unnecessarily, and don't ignore the

INJURY	SYMPTOMS	TREATMENT
Asphyxiation	Lips, ear lobes, blue; breathing stopped; unconscious.	Move to fresh air; give artificial respiration.
Bleeding *(from Arteries)*	Spurting, bright red blood from wounds.	Cover with pressure bandage. Apply hand pressure to nearest pressure point. Use tourniquet only when other methods fail to stop blood. Once applied, tourniquet should not be released except by a physician or nurse.
Bleeding *(from Veins)*	Steady flow; dark red blood.	Apply sterile compress firmly over wound to aid clotting.
Bleeding *(Internal)*	Pale face; faintness; thirst, sighing; weak, rapid pulse.	Lay with head low; apply cold packs to point you think bleeding.
Burns *(Thermal)*	Redness; pain; blisters; charred or cooked tissue.	Exclude air by applying burn spray or ointment or cover with dry bandage.
Burns *(Chemical)*	Redness; pain.	Wash thoroughly eyes or skin with clean water for 10 to 15 minutes.
Drowning	Unconscious, not breathing.	Remove water; cleanse mouth; tongue forward. Loosen clothing. Give artificial respiration.
Dislocations	Deformity compared to uninjured limb. Pain.	Dress in lines of deformity. Do not reduce.
Electric Shock	Unconscious; breathing stopped; burns at contact point.	Insulate self and rescue victim. Give artificial respiration. Dress burns.

INJURY	SYMPTOMS	TREAMENT
Fainting	Unconscious; face pale; cold sweat; pulse weak and rapid.	Lay with head low; keep warm; loosen clothing; give inhalant.
Fractures *(Simple)*	Pain; swelling; deformity; inability to move limb.	Support above and below fracture; apply well-padded splints.
Fractures *(Compound)*	Open wound; possibly bone protruding; bleeding.	Compress to wound; apply splints padded to deformity; do not set.
Fractures *(Skull)*	Possible bleeding eyes, nose and mouth; serum from ears in basal fracture.	Raise head; dress wound; no stimulants; keep warm and quiet.
Frost Bite	Affected part is white; no sensation.	Thaw slowly with lukewarm (not hot) water or by gently wrapping in warm blanket or clothes. Make patient warm as possible. If conscious, give warm drink.
Gas Poisoning *(Carbon Monoxide)*	Yawning; giddiness; weariness; throbbing heart.	Move to fresh air; give artificial respiration.
Heat Exhaustion	Pale face; cold sweat; weak pulse; shallow breathing.	Keep warm; rub limbs toward heart; give stimulants.
Shock	Pale face; cold sweat; dazed condition; partly or totally unconscious.	Lay with head low; keep warm; rub limbs; give stimulants if conscious.
Snake Bite	Pain; swelling; fang marks.	Apply tourniquet above bite; open fang marks lengthwise; use suction. Keep quiet.
Sunstroke	Unconscious; face flushed; skin hot and dry; breathing labored; pulse rapid.	Raise head; reduce body temperature with cold packs; no stimulants.

chance that he may be in shock. Know where pressure points are located (See illustration) so you can check arterial bleeding immediately.

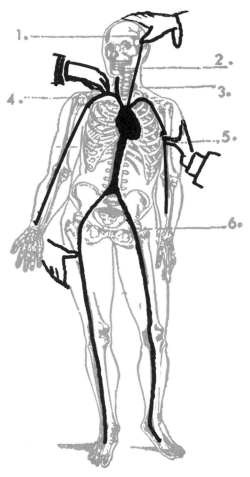

The arteries and pressure points.

If a victim's heart has stopped, or breathing ceases, use the heart-lung method approved by John Hopkins University School of Medicine and is taught to Fire, Police, Ambulance drivers and rescue squads across the country. Doctors use it in emergencies!!! The heart-lung method combines mouth-to-mouth respiration with closed-chest heart massage for cardiac arrest. If victim's breathing has ceased but heart is still beating, use the mouth-to-mouth method. If victim's heart has stopped, use the combination of mouth-to-mouth type of respiration with closed-chest heart massage.

This method has been effective in many cases of natural heart attacks, and dramatic results have been obtained in reviving persons seemingly dead of drowning, asphyxiation, electrical shock, suffocation, choking, and asthmatic attacks. Care must be used when applying closed heart massage, or internal injuries could result. The same applies when using the back-pressure arm-lift method of respiration. In cases of heart stoppage (cardiac arrest), best results may be had if two persons apply the heart-lung method, one first aider applying the mouth-to-mouth technique, while the other carries on with the closed chest heart massage. This is the way to apply this new method of respiration:

- Check pulse. Clear victim's mouth and air passages.

- Pinch victim's nose closed and forcibly breathe four or five deep breaths into his lungs until you note chest is expanded each time.

- Massage heart region once a second fifteen times (note illustration).

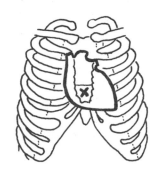

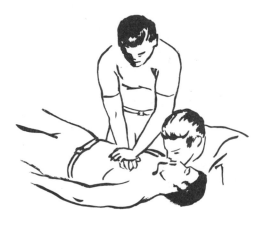

The heart-lung resuscitation technique.

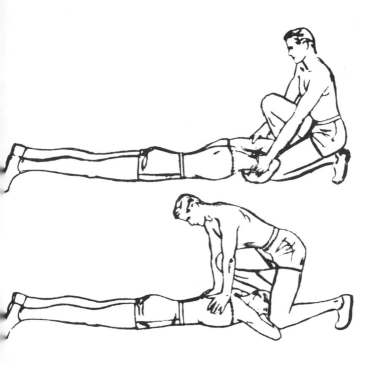

Mouth-to-mouth rescue breathing.
Arm-lift — shoulder-blade-pressure method of
resuscitation.

- Blow two or three quick breaths into mouth. Resume heart massage, interrupting it for mouth-to-mouth breathing every fifteen seconds.

- In simple cases of resuscitation where the heart has not stopped, the back-pressure arm-lift may be used or, better still, straight mouth-to-mouth technique (see illustrations).

In the arm-lift, 60 to 80 thrusts per minute are recommended; in mouth-to-mouth technique, use 12 to 20 breaths per minute. Watch the victim carefully when natural breathing starts — it may stop again. In that case continue resuscitation! Keep action up until the patient has recovered or is pronounced dead.

Bandaging an Injury

It pays to know how to bandage an injury properly. The illustrations show types of bandages and splints for various areas of the body.

First-Aid Kits

You can make up your own first-aid kit or buy one of the packaged ones available. Some of the latter are a bit bulky for a single knapsacker but would be fine for two or more, or for trips with pack animals. If you prefer to make up your own, the following list source Office of Civil Defense Disaster Services is for a family of four persons or less. Assemble the items, wrap them in a moisture-proof covering, and place them in an easily carried box. Paste this list to the box cover and keep the box in an easily accessible place.

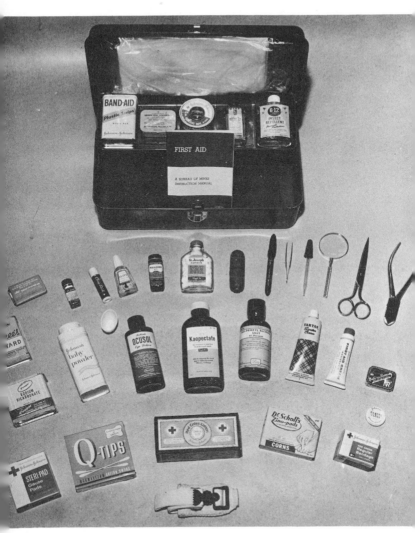

First-aid kit.

FOR THESE PURPOSES	USE THESE	OR THESE	SUGGESTED QUANTITY
For open wounds, scratches, and cuts. Not for burns.	1. Antiseptic solution: Benzalkonium Chloride Solution, U.S. P., 1 to 1,000 parts of water.	Quaternary ammonium compounds in water. Sold under trade names as Zephiran, Phemerol, Ceepryn, and Bactine.	3- to 6-oz. bottle.
For faintness, adult dose ½ teaspoon in cup of water; children 5 to 10 drops in ½ glass of water. As smelling salts, remove stopper, hold bottle under nose.	2. Aromatic spirits of ammonia.		1- to 2-oz. bottle.
For shock — dissolve 1 teaspoonful salt and ½ teaspoonful baking soda in 1 quart water. Have patient drink as much as he will. Don't give to unconscious person or semiconscious person. If using substitutes dissolve six 10-gr. sodium chloride tablets and six 5-gr. sodium bicarbonate (or sodium citrate) tablets in 1 qt. water.	3. Table salt.	Sodium chloride tablets, 10 gr., 50 tablets in bottle.	1 box.
	4. Baking soda.	Sodium bicarbonate or sodium citrate tablets, 5 gr., 50 tablets in bottle.	8- to 10-oz. box.
For a sling; as a cover; for a dressing.	5. Triangular bandage, folded, 37 by 37 by 52 in., with 2 safety pins.	Muslin or other strong material. Cut to exact dimensions. Fold and wrap each bandage and 2 safety pins separately in paper.	4 bandages.
For open wounds or for dry dressings for burns. These are packaged sterile.	6. Two medium first aid dressings, folded, sterile with gauze enclosed cotton pads, 8 in. by 7½ in. Packaged with muslin bandage and 4 safety pins.	a) Two emergency dressings 8 in. by 7½ in., in glassine bags, sterilized. One roller bandage, 2 in. by 10 yds. b) Four large sanitary napkins, wrapped separately and sterilized. One roller bandage, 2 in. by 10 yds.	As indicated.
For open wounds or for dry dressings for burns. These are packaged sterile.	7. Two small first aid dressings, folded, sterile with gauze enclosed cotton pads and gauze bandage, 4 in. by 7 in.	Twelve sterile gauze pads in individual packages, 3 in. by 3 in. One roller bandage, 1 in. by 10 yds.	As indicated.

Use	Item	Substitute	Quantity
For eyes irritated by dust, smoke, or fumes. Use 2 drops in each eye. Apply cold compresses every 20 minutes if possible.	8. Eye drops.	Bland eye drops sold by druggists under various trade names.	½- to 1-oz. bottle with dropper.
For splinting broken fingers or other small bones and for stirring solutions.	9. Twelve tongue blades, wooden.	Shingles, pieces of orange crate, or other light wood cut to approximately 1½ in. by 6 in.	As indicated.
For purifying water when it cannot be boiled. (Radioactive contamination cannot be neutralized or removed by boiling or by disinfectants.)	10. Water purification tablets Iodine (trade names—Globaline, Bursoline, Potable Aqua) Chlorine (trade name — Halazone).	Tincture of iodine or iodine solution (3 drops per quart of water.) Household bleach (approx. 5% available chlorine) 3 drops per quart of water.	Tablets — Bottle of 50 or 100. Liquid — One small bottle.
For bandages or dressings: Old soft towels and sheets are best. Cut in sizes necessary to cover wounds. Towels are burn dressings. Place over burns and fasten with triangular bandage or strips of sheet. Towels and sheets should be laundered, ironed, and packaged in heavy paper. Relaunder every 3 months.	11. Large bath towels.		2.
	12. Small bath towels.		2.
	13. Bed sheet.		1.
For administering stimulants and liquids.	14. Paper drinking cups.		25 to 50.
Electric lights may go out. Wrap batteries separately in moistureproof covering. Don't keep in flashlight.	15. Flashlight.		1.
	16. Flashlight batteries.		3.
For holding bandages in place.	17. Safety pins, 1½ in. long.		12 to 15.
For cutting bandages and dressings, or for removing clothing from injured body surface.	18. Razor blades, single edge.	Sharp knife or scissors.	3.
For cleansing skin.	19. Toilet soap.	Any mild soap.	1 bar.
For measuring or stirring solutions.	20. Measuring spoons.	Inexpensive plastic or metal.	1 set.
For splinting broken arms or legs.	21. Twelve splints, plastic or wooden, ⅛ to 1¼ in. thick, 3½ in. wide by 12 to 15 in. long.	A 40-page newspaper folded to dimensions, pieces of orange crate sidings, or shingles cut to size.	As indicated.

Insect Bites

Beware of insects when you get up in the morning, especially in the desert. Shake out your shoes, clothing, and hat, just in case you have had an overnight visitor. Some of the insects to avoid are poisonous spiders such as the black widow and recluse and tarantula, scorpions and centipedes, chiggers and itch mites, and ticks. Ticks can transmit spotted fever as well as tularemia.

Snake Bites

Of the over 40,000 snake bite cases that occur throughout the world, over 7,000 are reported in the United States. If you are careful and watch where you step, sit, and put your hands, you probably will never be bitten. In fact, it is very likely that you will never see a poisonous snake on your trip. However, most snakes of this type feed at night, so be careful when going to the latrine after dark. Use a flashlight and wear your shoes when walking over to the toilet pit.

Snake-Bite Kit. There are several snake-bite kits on the market which can be obtained at most drug stores. Three of the best known are: The Cutter Snakebite Kit, Cutter Laboratories, Berkeley, California; the antivenin syringe-type kit of Wyeth Laboratories, Inc., Marietta, Pennsylvania. Most of the go-light backpackers whom I have seen carrying such a kit take the famous small (about the size of a shotgun shell) Cutter kit with three plastic suction cups. Full instructions for use come with each kit and should be read carefully *before* the trip is begun.

Small snakebite kit. Courtesy Cutter Laboratories.

Avoid Traveling Alone

Generally it is good advice not to travel alone. However, if you do travel alone, be extra careful! And be sure that you have left word where you are going and when you will be back, so that in case of delay due to accident, someone will be alerted to the possibility of danger. Stay on the trail, for if you short-cut or travel cross country, it can be time-consuming and perhaps impossible for a rescue team to find you. In any event, traveling alone can be hazardous. Even experienced

Four-hand carry. Two rescuers can make a four-handed seat on which to carry a conscious victim. Each rescuer steadies the victim with an arm around his back. Then each rescuer slips his other arm under the victim's thighs and clasps the other's wrist. One pair of arms makes a seat rest, the other pair a back rest. Both rescuers then rise slowly in unison, lifting the victim from the ground.

hikers sometimes slip, trip and fall, and injure themselves — often far from medical aid. In a group it is usually possible to carry an injured person — at least to a comfortable site to await rescue. The illustration shows a useful four-hand carry.

Don't Become a Winter Casualty

Many of us can recall the expression, "chilled to the bone." Many outdoorsmen are not aware of this dangerous chill factor, which must be taken into account in the mountains, or elsewhere generally during late October to the middle of March. Chill factor is a term used to identify a condition which results when temperature and wind are combined. The usual effect is always a lower equivalent temperature than that which the thermometer indicates — so *beware,* it can kill you if you are caught far from quick shelter! In spite of warm clothing, the peril exists for thousands who participate in outdoor winter activities in our recreation areas. For many fortunately, the results are not so catastrophic. Persons exposed to a moderate chill factor situation may experience only extreme discomfort. As temperatures drop and winds increase, the problem can turn critical in a very few minutes.

How to Check. If you are planning a hike in a cold area check with your local weather bureau or Coast Guard station and find out what wind conditions may be expected for the day. If you are already in the field and the temperature continues to drop, watch out for any increase in wind, head immediately for the nearest shelter as quickly as possible if the wind picks up.

By predicting the amount of wind chill you can avoid becoming another winter victim. This is relatively easy to do. The United States Weather Bureau will furnish up-to-date weather data information, and hourly forecasts are available any time of the day or night. Make a note of the predicted winds and temperatures, and then apply these figures to the Wind-chill Chart shown here. This chart was developed for use by Park and Forest Rangers who patrol the winter scene, men well aware of winter hazards. The chart is simple to use. First locate the existing (or predicted) temperature on top of the horizontal line. Next, find the existing (or predicted) wind velocity in the vertical column on the far left under the heading Wind Speed (m.p.h.). Now follow the line of figures down from Local Temperature and across from Wind Speed. The equivalent temperature is at the point where the two lines intersect. For example, a reading of −4 degrees on the top horizontal line and a wind speed of 25 m.p.h. on the left vertical line intersect gives an equivalent temperature of 50 degrees below zero! (A free wind-chill chart may be

WIND SPEED	LOCAL TEMPERATURE (F)										
	32	23	14	5	-4	-13	-22	-31	-40	-49	-58
5	29	20	10	1	-9	-18	-28	-37	-47	-56	-65
10	18	7	-4	-15	-26	-37	-48	-59	-70	-81	-92
15	13	-1	-13	-25	-37	-49	-61	-73	-85	-97	-109
20	7	-6	-19	-32	-44	-57	-70	-83	-96	-109	-121
25	3	-10	-24	-37	-50	-64	-77	-90	-104	-117	-130
30	1	-13	-27	-41	-54	-68	-82	-97	-109	-123	-137
35	-1	-15	-29	-43	-57	-71	-85	-99	-113	-127	-142
40	-3	-17	-31	-45	-59	-74	-87	-102	-116	-131	-145
45	-3	-18	-32	-46	-61	-75	-89	-104	-118	-132	-147
50	-4	-18	-33	-47	-62	-76	-91	-105	-120	-134	-148

For Properly Clothed Persons	Little Danger	Considerable Danger	Very Great Danger

DANGER FROM FREEZING OF EXPOSED FLESH

Wind-chill chart.

obtained from Information Office, Bombardier, Ltd., Decarie Blvd., Montreal, Quebec, Canada. Included is information on how to dress properly to withstand winter cold.)

Another point you must remember is: if you are moving through air as you do when sailing an iceboat, skiing, or operating a snowmobile, you should always remember to figure in the approximate speed of your means of transportation, and this which will add more cold chill factors to the above figures.

Snow surveyors and others who travel or patrol the winter backcountry heed the winter wind-chill factors to survive cold weather sickness, injuries or death, and so can the winter sportsman!

The Pacific Crest Trail

The Long Long Trail

First, what is a wilderness trail? The dictionary describes it as a rough way made or worn through woods, or across mountains, prairies, or other untraveled regions; a path or track made across a wild area, over rough country, or the like, by the passage of men or animals. The Pacific Crest Trail is just that!

This wild trail extends through the states of Washington, Oregon, and California and is divided into eight sections. It reaches from the Canadian border southward for 2,313 miles to its end at the international boundary marker No. 251 on the Mexican border — near the town of Campo in San Diego County.

Westward Ho

Much has been written about the 2,000-mile-long Appalachian Trail in the East, with its early history and its greatest elevation of 6,641 feet, at Clingman's Dome in the Great Smokies. However, the really "big one" — the Pacific Crest Trail System — is the longest trail in

The Pacific Crest Trail.

this nation. It is 313 miles longer than the Appalachian, and it is the only border-to-border trail existing so far in the United States. Not only does it slightly outrank the Appalachian Trail in length, but it doubles it in elevation, with a record 13,200 feet along the High Sierra section of the John Muir Trail. It crosses 25 National Forests and 12 National Forest Wildernesses and links together 7 National Parks. Its route traverses 19 major canyons, reaches some 900 lakes, and surmounts 57 major mountain passes.

The Pacific Crest Trail as a continuous trail (pathway) is not yet complete. The early exploration parties (1935-1938) demonstrated that experienced persons could make their way through wilderness areas and along summit crests following a list of landmarks for the route. At the present time because of development of recreation areas in the National Forests and National Parks it is deemed advisable to change the route in some locations from the early Pacific Crest Trail System Conference projections in order to now establish the Pacific Crest Trail System in as much wilderness country as possible and still reach recreation areas in State and National Parks and in National Forests.

The route now under study will lengthen the trail from 2,313 miles to 2,404 miles. The Trail is now projected across private lands, National Forests, National Parks, Bureau of Land Management land and State land and Parks. Of the route now under consideration 1,910 miles are on Federal Land, 42 miles are on State Land, and 452 miles are across private land. Rights-of-way will need to be obtained across private lands before the Trail can be completed from Canada to Mexico. The National Trails System Act does not permit government condemnation of private land for

*Hikers camp at Cascade Pass in Mt. Baker
National Forest.*

trail use. Some money is available for purchase of private land for trail use.

There are now 695 miles of the Trail in Washington and Oregon with an additional 255 miles in these States to be constructed. In California there are 790 miles of the Trail with 274 miles more of "present detour" trails, and an additional 400 miles of the route along Forest roads at the present time.

Best Travel Periods. Normally, the best time to travel any section of the Pacific Crest Trail is between July 1 and September 1. In any case, it is best to first check with the district ranger in the area where you plan to travel. You can contact the ranger by phone or mail.

Carry Everything With You. The backpacker must be prepared to travel several days between supply points. An occasional Forest Guard station or government camp can be found along the trail, but there is no provision for sale of supplies at these locations. Therefore, Pacific Crest Trail travelers should be prepared to be entirely dependent upon their own resources.

Much of the pleasure of any trip depends on the proper planning. Annoyances and disappointments sometimes mar a trek because the plan was incomplete — some little item forgotten. *Don't* forget essentials such as matches, salt, soap, or toilet tissue. Many do

Walking with a backpack is probably the simplest and most economical, though slowest, method of travel. Of necessity, the pack will consist of the correct amount of food, camping gear and a frame pack to carry the outfit. Don't forget a lightweight tent or tarpaulin and rain gear. A frame pack or rucksack will be more handy than a packboard. Because the trail traverses terrain that lies at high altitudes, take warm clothing!

Fire Danger! Much of the beauty of all sections of

*View over Luna Lake and glacial moraines in the
Skagit Rangers District of the North Cascade
Primitive Area, Mt. Baker National Forest.*

the Pacific Crest Trail lies in the magnificent alpine forest it winds through. Fire will destroy this beauty. The hiking camper should remember that he is in a country which is relatively inaccessible to the firefighting organizations of both the Park and National Forest Services. Particular care *must* be used with fire in the forest at all times!

Fire Tools Necessary. When saddle and pack train travelers or hikers leading pack stock pass through the National Forests, the following fire tools are required: (a) one axe with handle not less than 26 inches long; (b) one long-handled shovel with a blade not less than 8 inches wide; and (c) one water container with a capacity of 1 gallon or more (a folding canvas bucket is a good bet). Remember, those who call the forests "home" are counting on *you* to put out your campfire!

Warning about Bears and Other Animals. Avoid sow bears, especially when they have cubs. Keep away from cubs or you are in trouble! If you see one or more cubs, you can be sure the mother is close by. Play it safe and detour widely around these animals. A wise hiker will also leave skunks and porcupines alone. And he will examine himself at least twice a day for ticks. Ticks are annoying, and some species carry Rocky Mountain fever.

About Motor Vehicles on the Trail. Since the trails are not designed for motorized equipment, scooters and motorcycles are not recommended. They are prohibited in Primitive and Wilderness Areas of the National Forests and on the trails of the National Parks.

Limited Pasturage. It is advisable to carry horse-feed, as there are many areas where forage is limited, especially during the latter part of the summer. Check with the local ranger regarding these sections.

Communications. Communication with the outside world is not easy while you are en route along the trail. Telephones are available at only a few points. The map shows a few resorts, fire lookout, and patrol stations equipped with emergency telephones or radios. The mountain resorts, besides furnishing meals, lodging, baths, boats, etc., have camp supplies in stock.

U. S. Forest Service Trail Logs

There is more to this trail walking sport than just dumping a bulky old sleeping bag and some beans into a Boy Scout knapsack and heading for the hills. You will need some hiking intelligence as well as some backpacking logistics. Backpacking logistics is the science concerned with the transportation of the supplies and equipment that you will carry on your own back, or on that of a burro or other pack animal that you lead along (see Chapters 3 and 9).

Now that you have found out, in Chapter 2, where to obtain maps and trail information, here is one method of finding out how far you live from a hiking and camping area near you. Use your town or city as a hub, then on a road map draw a circle out from it — one hour's driving time, about 50 miles out; 100 miles, two hours; 150 miles, three hours; 200 miles, four hours drive, and so on as far as you want to go. You will be surprised at the amount of hiking paths and trails you will find within one of these circles. There may be a state park, or a National Park, Forest, or Recreational Area near your home.

A trail log will come in handy. It will tell you what to expect along the route, distances between points,

Looking southwest from Hannegan Pass in the
Glacier Ranger District of Mt. Baker National
Forest.

elevations, place names, camping spots, and various regulations. In this chapter are examples of the U. S. Forest Service's Logs for the famous Cascade Crest Trail and Oregon Skyline Trail, with accompanying maps. They take you through scenic Washington to the Oregon border and then along the volcanic splendors to the Oregon peaks to the California state line. (No such map and log combination is available for the California section, as it is not actually a straight-line trail.)

In following the trail log at home, in camp, or along the trail, keep in mind that the Pacific Crest Trail System — Canada to Mexico — is continually being worked on in various sections, so there will always be a few inaccuracies in the maps. A few trail sections will have been changed from their locations on the map and rerouted to safer, better, or more scenic locations, or they will have been altered because of slides, washouts, or other damage. There are still a number of sections of this trail where no actual trail exists — the hiker must either go cross-country or make wide detours over other trails, or follow a combination of both — but these stretches are being steadily worked on to conform to Pacific Crest Trail standards.

THE CASCADE CREST TRAIL

Canadian Border to Columbia River. This portion of the Pacific Crest Trail follows the backbone of the Cascade Range for a distance of 457 miles; it passes through five National Forests: Mt. Baker, Okanogan, Wenachee, Snoqualmie, and Gifford Pinchot. The trail also crosses four wilderness areas: North Cascades, Glacier Peak, Goat Rocks, and Mount Adams; and it skirts the east boundary of Mt. Rainier National Park.

In its windings through this scenic area, it penetrates a primitive America, refreshing and invigorating to the imagination. The foot traveler can gaze not only on the dormant volcanoes of Mt. Adams, Mt. St. Helens, Mt. Rainier, Glacier Peak, and Mt. Baker, but he can see a spectacular display of glaciation, both past and present. There are 519 glaciers covering 97 square miles between Snoqualmie Pass and the Canadian border.

The North and South Ends

The north end of the Cascade Crest Trail begins at Monument No. 83 on Trail No. 482 at the Canadian border. This point is reached by a trail open to foot and horse travel only from E. C. Manning Provincial Park in Canada. Alternate Trail No. 482 joins the Cascade Crest Trail at Castle Pass.

For trail information in Manning Park, write to: Ranger, British Columbia Forest Service, E. C. Manning Park, British Columbia, Canada.

The south end of the Cascade Crest Trail begins at U. S. Highway No. 830, 56 miles east of Vancouver, Washington. To go from the south end of the Cascade Trail and enter the Oregon Skyline Trail, one should cross the Columbia River at the "Bridge of The Gods," or at the Hood River bridge. It is possible to drive closer to Mt. Adams, up Wind River via U. S. Highway No. 8C and Carson-Guler Road N 60. This would cut 27 miles off the Crest Trail.

An automobile may be used to cut off several days' walking time at either end of the trip, or it may be used to meet the traveler at selected points between. The trail crosses several modern highways and four railroads. These roadways offer many and varied opportunities for shorter skyline trips to those who do not have time for the full journey from the Canadian border to the Columbia River.

It will be noted on the map that there are a few alternate routes. Others will be added in the future. Scores of short trails lead to nearby alpine lakes and other wilderness features, as well as down in to the valley below. The large lakes have excellent fishing and nearly all the smaller ones on or near the Trail have been stocked with rainbow, eastern brook, or other species of trout. Mountain goats inhabit the highest and most rugged terrain. A few mountain sheep and elk can be seen occasionally, blacktail deer are common on the ridges and creek bottoms to the west; mule deer travel the country east of the summits. Black bear are plentiful, especially in the huckleberry patches during late summer.

Obtaining Maps, Locating Packers and Outfitters

It should be pointed out that Forest Supervisors in charge of the five National Forests through which the Cascade Crest Trail passes will provide maps and give travelers information regarding packers and outfitters who are equipped to handle trail parties of three or more persons. However arrangements for packers should be made well in advance. The Cascade Crest National Forests, in order, are:

Okanogan — P.O. Box 950, Okanogan 98840
Mount Baker — P.O. Box 845, Bellingham 98225
Wenatchee — P.O. Box 811, Wenatchee 98801
Snoqualmie — 919 2nd Ave., Seattle 98104
Gifford Pinchot—P.O. Box 449, Vancouver 98660

Maps and Log — Cascade Crest Trail

The maps and log illustrated here show by legend and symbol various improvements of interest to the trail traveler and are a guide to the trail. There are a few improved camps along the route. The backpacker should remember that he is in wild country and will probably find no accommodations except wood and water and perhaps a few rough fireplaces and primitive tables some woodsman has built. Most meals will have to be eaten from the lap, a rock, or log. Where the trail traverses the west side of the Cascade Range, running streams are generally plentiful and there are many camping spots to choose from. East of the main divide, the Trail passes through a drier region, but there is still water for camping.

THE OREGON SKYLINE TRAIL —
Columbia River to California Border

The Skyline Trail Route

The Oregon Skyline Trail is appropriately named. From the time it climbs out of the Columbia River Gorge it follows the skyline of the Cascades across the state of Oregon, for a distance of over 406 miles at altitudes from 4,000 to 7,100 feet. This Oregon section of the Pacific Crest Trail begins at the Columbia River near Bonneville Dam. It winds southward high over the flanks of 11,245 foot Mt. Hood. Mt. Hood is said to be the most frequently climbed snow-capped mountain after Japan's Fujiyama. However, a few of us old-time mountain climbers will dispute this. The trail snakes

At Cascade Locks take Frontage Road east
3 mi. to:

		ASTERISKS ON MAP	LINE NORTH
0	**COLUMBIA GORGE WORK CENTER. POINT "A"**	0	374
	7 mi. across Herman Creek. 1 mi. Jct. #405 Ruckle Creekway (west). ¼ mi. west to campsite, water, horsefeed. 3 mi. Jct. #434 Eagle Skyline Trail (west). Jct. N-20 Larch Mountain Road (east). Take trail to west of road. 1 mi. to:		
13	**WAHTUM LAKE.** Improved campground. Jct. #440 Eagle Creek Trail (west). This is alternate trail from Eagle Creek Recreation Area near Bonneville Dam (13-1/2 miles).	13	361
	3 mi. Indian Springs. Improved campground. 2 mi. Jct. N-20 Larch Mountain Road (trail crosses road). 4 mi. #615 Buck Point Trail; viewpoint ¼ mi. west. 3 mi. to:		
25	**LOST LAKE.** Jct. Trail #617. Lake 1-1/2 mi. east. Improved campground, Forest Service Station.	12	349
	4 mi. to:		
29	**LOLO PASS.** Elevation 3400. Jct. N18 Lolo Pass Road. Zigzag 12 mi. west.	4	345
	3 mi. to:		
32	**JCT. #600 TIMBERLINE TRAIL** (from east). Campsite.	3	342
	2 mi. Campsite. Jct. #797 Portage Trail (west). 1½ mi. Ramona Falls. Shelter. ½ mi. Jct. #770 Sandy River Trail (west). ½ mi. Sandy River Crossing. Use caution. 4-1/2 mi. to:		
41	**PARADISE PARK.** Campsite, and mountain meadows. Jct. #776 East Zigzag Mountain Trail (west). Jct. #778 Paradise Park Trail (west).	9	333
	2½ mi. Jct. #779 Hidden Lake Trail (west). 1-1/2 mi. to:		
45	**TIMBERLINE LODGE.** Restaurant, lodging, swimming, pool, nearby campgrounds.	4	329
	1½ mi. Jct. #600 Timberline Trail (east). 3½ mi. Barlow Pass. Jct. Oregon State Highway #35, (east and west). 4 mi. Twin Lakes. Campsite, fishing. 2 mi. to:		
56	**WAPINITIA PASS.** Elevation 3,949. **POINT "B"**	11	318

Sample log — Cascade Crest Trail.

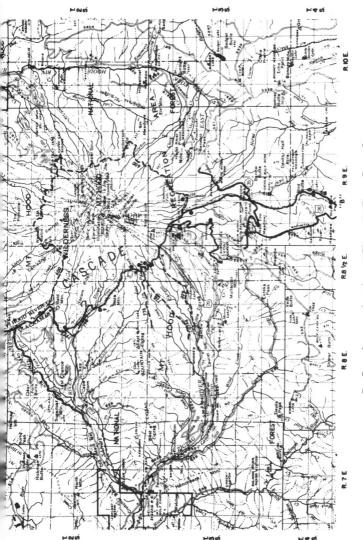

B. Sample map (sections "C" to "B".) — Cascade Crest Trail.

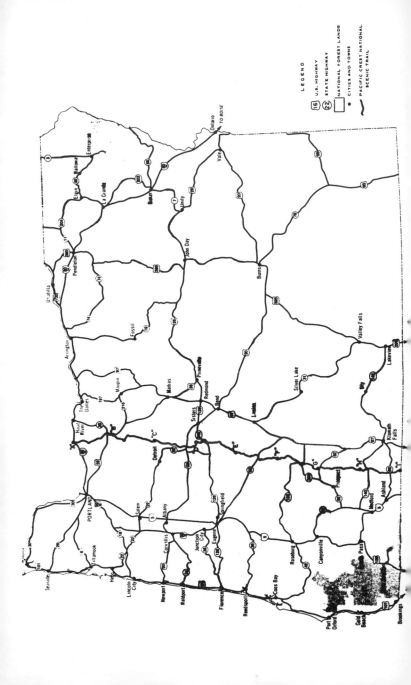

GENERAL TRAIL LOG

A – B   56 miles

This portion of the Pacific Crest National Scenic Trail opens in late June and at higher elevations closes approximately mid-October. With the exception of the Bald Mountain area, water is generally available from springs and small creeks all along the trail. Herman Creek and Sandy River are dangerous in high water. Occasionally sandy sections due to glacial action offer some hazard. Best camping spots are at Wahtum Lake, Lost Lake, Paradise Park, Ramona Falls, Phlox Point, and Twin Lakes. Signing is good all along the trail. Stores for some supplies are available at Lost Lake and Government Camp.

B – C   48 miles

The northern portion of this section is generally open in mid-June; the southern portion is not open until mid-July, with snow still in some portions. The trail usually closes by mid-October. Water is generally available. Boggy trail tread in the Warm Springs River area may offer some difficulty to horse travel early in the season. Good camping spots are generally available. Signing is good. Some supplies are available from a store at Olallie Lake Campground.

C – D   47 miles

This portion of the trail opens approximately July 15 and normally closes by October 1. Water is available at Breitenbush Lake. There are some snow-fed streams available in the Jefferson Park area. This portion of the trail occasionally is temporarily in poor condition due to extremely wet weather. Signing is good except on snowfield near Mt. Jefferson, which should be crossed in the daytime only.

Campsites are few between Pamelia Lake and Santiam Pass with no horsefeed. Russell Creek crossing may be temporarily in poor condition early in the season because of slides and sloughs during the winter. Travelers are advised to contact the District Ranger at Detroit if using this section prior to August 1.

D – E   48 miles

Four miles of rough, abrasive trail are in lava rock south of saddle between Mt. Washington and McKenzie Pass. Many good camping spots with horsefeed from Linton Creek Trail junction south to Sisters Mirror Lake, and from Horse Lake to Reserve Meadow. This section of trail is in good condition for both foot and horse travel and is adequately signed.

Snow usually blocks the trail until about July 10, but a few snow banks will be encountered until the end of July. Trail is well signed. Snow closes the trail about October 15. Snowstorms can be expected any time after September 15. In the fall, travelers should be prepared for cold, wet weather. Unimproved camping places are numerous. Horsefeed is limited along the southern portion of this section. Suggest lake water be boiled before drinking.

E – F   43 miles

Campsites with horsefeed available adjacent to Irish, Taylor, and Charlton Lakes, and at Douglas Horse Pasture. Trail is in good condition and is adequately signed.

General condition of trail from Rosary Lakes to Windigo Pass is good. Some hazard may be encountered in fording Trapper Creek on horseback. There is a bridge for hikers.

Good campsites and horsefeed are available after July 15. Normally the trail is open by July 10 and usually remains open into October.

F – G   46 miles

The section from Windigo Pass to Crater Lake National Park is in good, safe, usable condition and is well marked. Drinking water is available only at Tombstone Mine, Tolo Camp, Maidu Lake, and Upper Thielsen Creek Crossing. Horsefeed is very limited. Trail is not free of snow until late July and usually closes early in October.

past 10,400-foot Mt. Jefferson, Three Fingered Jack and 7,802 foot Mt. Washington. Geologists believe that lava flows in the Mt. Washington Wilderness are from eruptions recent enough to have been witnessed by human eyes within the past 1,000 years.

Odell Lake and Lakeview Mountain in Deschutes National Forest.

After passing the Belknap lava area and the beautiful 10,000-foot Three Sisters peaks, the trail meanders through a scenic lake region including Waldo, Odell, Crescent, and Diamond Lakes. Further south, it goes through Crater Lake National Park and along the uppermost crest to Fourmile Lake east of Mt. McLoughlin, and then past Lake of the Woods to cross Highway 66 near the southern end of the Cascade Range.

The Crest Trial is generally more accessible for shorter trips in Oregon than in Washington. This is particularly true in the North Cascades.

The forest and park regulations are similar to those in the Cascade Crest Trail region. This interesting section of the Pacific Crest Trail, the Oregon Skyline Trail passes through six national forests and also Crater Lake National Park. In this most scenic stretch of winding trail, the hiker will also cross six different Wilderness Areas within the National Forests — there are wilderness and primitive highlands where travel is only allowed on foot, horseback, or pack horse. They are: Mt. Hood, Jefferson, Mt. Washington, Three Sisters, Diamond Peak and Mountain Lakes.

National Forests crossed by the Oregon Skyline Trail are:

Mt. Hood — P. O. Box 16040, Portland 97216

Williamette — P. O. Box 1272, Eugene 97401

Deschutes — P. O. Box 751, Bend 97701

Umpqua — P. O. Box 1008, Roseburg 97470

Rogue River — P. O. Box 520, Medford 97501

Winema — P. O. Box 1390, Klamath Falls 97601

Hikers in Willamette National Forest view the North and Middle Sisters.

CALIFORNIA TO MEXICO

Not A Straight-Line Trail

The 1,464 miles of the California portion of the Pacific Crest Trail are not a straight-line trail as in Washington and Oregon. Its five sections run through 14 National Forests and are made up of already existing roads and trails which go in a generally north-south direction. In this way it is similar to the Appalachian Trail.

Maps, regulations, and other information are available from the various National Forest headquarters. Some National Parks also publish maps featuring local side trails and points of interest.

National Forests in California crossed by the Pacific Crest Trail are:

Klamath — 1215 South Main St., Yreka 96097

Shasta-Trinity — 1615 Continental St., Redding 96001

Lassen — 707 Nevada St., Susanville 96130

Plumas — 500 Lawrence St., Quincy 95971

Tahoe — Highway 40 and Coyote St. Nevada City 95959

Eldorado — 100 Forni Road, Placerville 95667

Toiyabe — Main Post Office Bldg., Reno, Nevada 89504

Inyo — 2957 Birch St., Bishop 93514

Sierra — Federal Bldg., 1130 "O" St. Fresno 93721

Sequoia — P. O. Box 391, Porterville 93258

Angeles — 1015 N. Lake St., Pasadena 91104

San Bernardino — 144 N. Mountain View San Bernardino 92401

Cleveland — 3211 Fifth Ave., San Diego 92103

The Pacific Crest Trail in California is travelable in its entirety, but only those experienced in high-mountain and arid-desert travel and camping would be able to do this without great difficulty. Temperatures in the desert sections range from extremely high in the summer to bitterly cold and windy in the winter. In the Sierras, high mountain passes may be closed by snow until late July and temperatures can drop rapidly to a cold low with a summer snowstorm. (I have seen six inches of snow at the 8,600-foot elevation in mid-July at Tuolumne Meadows. However, the snow melted and disappeared in a day or so and warm sun took over during the day.) Desert conditions can be dangerously demanding on the hiker too.

Looking down into Yosemite Valley, Yosemite National Park.

The Lava Crest Section

From Klamath Falls to Thousand Lake Wilderness, north of Lassen Volcanic National Park, the Trail circles in a westerly direction. It is routed partly to avoid the Tule Lake and Lower Klamath Falls Wildlife Refuge west of Merrill, Oregon (this bird stop is probably the most important one on the Pacific flyway) and partly to take in the exciting scenic country of the Marble Mountain Wilderness and Trinity Divide.

The Lava Crest Trail begins at the Oregon border ("I" on the Forest Service map of the Oregon Skyline Trail) and runs southward through the forested lava mountains of northern California for 339 miles to Yuba Gap.

The Tahoe-Yosemite Stretch

The Tahoe-Yosemite Trail is sierran and averages over 7,000 feet in elevation. It traverses the Tahoe National Forest across Bald Ridge through Desolation Valley Wilderness, five miles west of famous Lake Tahoe. This beautiful mountain lake is 1,646 feet deep at a surface altitude of 6,247 feet and it covers a water area of 195 square miles. The Trail winds along the east edge of Upper and Lower Blue Lakes and along the western edge of the Toiyabe National Forest and enters the Stanislaus National Forest. It passes through the Emigrant Basin Wilderness, entering Yosemite National Park at Bond's Pass. From there it moves into Tuolumne Meadows, where this section of trail ends. Distance is 239 miles, and travel time is about 13 to 15 days.

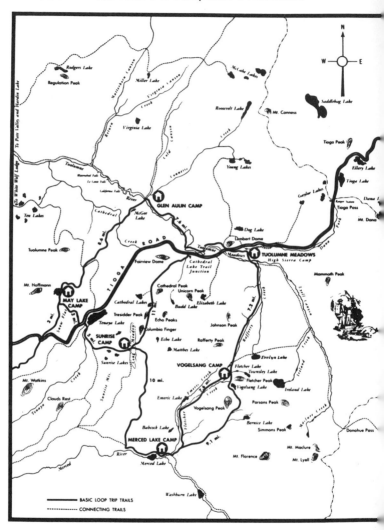

*Yosemite National Park map showing trail system,
tent, camps, and points of interest.*

The Famous John Muir Trail Section

The Sierra Nevada Range — a great mass of granite mountains featuring the famous Big Trees — begins in Yosemite National Park and culminates in the southern group of outstanding fourteen thousand-foot peaks at the headwaters of the Kings River and the Kern. Along this portion — between Yosemite and the Sierra Crest section of the trail — are an amazing number of high peaks; 306 are over 12,000 feet in elevation; 94 of them over 13,000 feet; and 11 of them towering beside the Pacific Crest Trail, are over 14,000 feet. This magnificent group is rightly called the "Top of the United States," and rivals the Alps of Europe. The king of this group is Mt. Whitney, 14,496 feet, highest of all peaks in this country outside of Alaska.

During storm periods, the lightning unleashed by convection storms against these mighty sierran heights is often extremely dangerous, and hikers and climbers should get off the high peaks and seek lower elevations for safety.

On the eastern side of this mighty range, the mountains drop off rapidly in elevation into Mono Basin and the Owens Valley. Forty miles eastward as the crow flies, from Mt. Whitney's 14,496-foot elevation, the land drops off to 282 feet below sea level, in Death Valley National Monument. On the western slope, the mountain range rises gradually from foothills to the mighty crest, so high mountain travel up and down the range and in proximity to the crest is more practical on the western side.

The John Muir Trail leaves Yosemite Valley, meanders over the Sunrise Trail, and connects onto the Pacific Crest Trail System at Tuolumne Meadows. The

Pacific Crest Trail follows the John Muir Trail southward, leaving the Yosemite National Park boundary at Donohue Pass (12,073 feet) and entering the Sierra National Forest, where it winds through the Thousand Island Lakes region, Mt. Dana-Minarets Area, Devil's Postpile National Monument on through the John Muir Wilderness Area and Sequoia National Forest. The Trail continues along through Evolution Valley and Kings Canyon National Park, over Muir Pass (12,059 feet), on into Sequoia National Park over Foresters Pass. The 13,200 foot Foresters Pass is distinguished as the "highest pass for man or beast," in the United States; stands on the east boundary of Sequoia National Park a few miles north of the giant Whitney group, and centers a magnificent grand array of major peaks well over 13,000, with Mt. Keith (13,990 feet) just 10 feet under the 14,000 foot group, rising out of the pass itself.

The view north, extending to the Palisades and beyond, is one of the most outstanding scenic panoramas in the world, and is comparable to that from Junction Pass (12,650 feet) a mile to the east. Those hardy hikers who want the best views can ascend Junction Peak (13,903 feet.), a short distance to the east, to feast their eyes on a panorama that is even more remarkable. This peak occupies a strategic position at the junction of the Sierra Crest and Kings-Kern Divide, offering an unobstructed view in all directions.

The panoramic view southward along the Sierra Crest includes the Whitney group of 14,000-foot mountains. Some of these peaks are, from the north to the south; Mt. Williamson (14,384 feet), just east of the Crest; Mt. Tyndall (14,025 feet), and, immediately west of Williamson; Mt. Barnard (14,003); Mt. Russell (14,190 feet), immediately north of Mt. Whitney; Mt. Whitney

*Backpackers in Kings Canyon National Park pass
a lake at 12,000 feet.*

(14,496 feet), southernmost point on the Sierra Crest reached by the John Muir Trail; Mt. Muir (14,025 feet); and Mt. Langley (14,042 feet). A short distance south, the range loses rapidly in altitude. Total traveling distance is 178 miles, and travel time is 20 to 25 days.

The Sierra Crest Trail

The Sierra Crest Trail extends southward for the next 137 miles from Mt. Whitney on over the Tehachapi Range to Tehachapi Pass. The Sierra Crest Trail, below the John Muir Trail, soon winds down from that part of the Sierra Nevada called "High Sierra." This stretch is primitive wilderness country for about the next 70 miles below Mt. Whitney and averages 7,000 feet altitude, with cool nights, high pine and fir forests, alpine lakes, streams and meadows. The next 90 miles show just the opposite in forest cover. This area is arid and the forest trees are thinly scattered; it is dry and slightly above what would be called semi-desert. The really dry trail begins at Cannell Meadows. The long jaunt down the backbone of America brings us at last to Tehachapi Pass. Distance is 137 miles and travel time for this section is 14 to 18 days.

The Desert Crest Trail

This desolate, but interesting section of the Pacific Crest Trail passes through the Mojave Desert and up over the Piute Mountains, where it enters the Angeles National Forest passing along the north boundary of

The spectacular 14,000-feet Sierra Divide and Palisade Glaciers are admired by hikers in the John Muir Wilderness Area, Inyo National Forest.

the Devil's Canyon - Bear Canyon Wilderness Area. It meanders through the Big Pines Recreation Area, enters the San Bernardino National Forest, and travels south of Lake Arrowhead along Big Bear Lake's north shore, then south through the San Gorgonio Wilderness Area. Here the trail begins to drop, but it picks up altitude again as it winds through the San Jacinto Wilderness and Game Refuge. Descending again, the trail crosses more desert terrain and passes through the Coahuila Indian Reservation. From here the trail crosses the Cleveland National Forest through the Agua Tibia Wilderness, and Mission Indian Reserve, Mesa Grande, and Santa Isabel Indian Reservations. Next it goes through the Cuyamaca State Park and Cuyapaipe, La Posta, and Campo Indian Reservations. It ends two miles south of Campo, California, on the Mexican border at international boundary marker No. 251.

Warning! Where the Pacific Crest Trail enters the Mojave and Sonoran Desert sections, summer temperatures in the shade range well over 120° F., and ground temperatures reach 156° F, plus! These portions of the Desert Crest Trail should only be traveled during the cool of night or during the day during the cooler months.

Campsites may be found approximately 15 miles apart. Water is uncertain over most of this area so all necessary water should be carried along on this trail, since springs and water holes may have dried up. *Don't* take a chance! A minimum of one gallon of water per day per person is required to keep from becoming dehydrated. A person traveling the desert in the summer months should drink his fill of water at every opportunity.

The Appalachian Trail

The Long Trail — East

The Appalachian Trail System of the eastern mountains is not an unbroken range as the Sierra Nevada tends to be; it is made up of successive mountain groups and roughly parallel ranges separated by valleys. Like the southern end of the Pacific Crest Trail in California, the Trail must sometimes follow highways and old tote roads in crossing valleys from one ridge or mountain to another. However, such use of roads and motorways is only a small fraction of the Trail System.

The North and South Terminus

The Appalachian Trail System is a continous path — for travel on foot — extending through the mountain wilderness of the Eastern Atlantic states. It is a skyline route along the crest of mountain ranges generally referred to as Appalachian — hence the name of this famous trail. The Trail extends from Mt. Katahdin (5,267 feet), a massive granite mountain in the central Maine wilderness, over 2,000 miles southward to

Springer Mountain in central Georgia. It traverses 14 states and finds its greatest elevation at 6,641 feet, at Clingman's Dome in the Great Smoky Mountains. The low point is only slightly above sea level where it crosses the Hudson River. The Trail was completed in 1937 when the last two miles were opened on the south slope of Mt. Sugarloaf in Maine. The southern terminus at the time was Mt. Oglethorpe, in Georgia. Major changes since then in several states have resulted in a more stabilized trail route through scenic and isolated areas. Every mile of this great trail has been marked and measured and it is open throughout its length.

The nature of the Trail is determined in some degree by the ownership of the area through which it passes. In the north, with the exception of the White and Green Mountain National Forests and some State Parks, the Trail route is privately owned. From the Shenandoah National Park south the crestline is for the most part publicly owned, either as a National Forest or a National Park. The Trail in Massachusetts, Connecticut, New York, and New Jersey frequently passes through small towns and is easily accessible by highway and railroad, permitting big city dwellers to use it for short or week-end trips.

The Maine Section

The Trail starts from the spectacular Mt. Katahdin, a solitary monarch in a wilderness of lake and forest in Central Maine, and meanders across the state for 280 miles, going through only two towns en route. These are convenient points for the backpacker to take on supplies and obtain accommodations if he so desires.

MT KATAHDIN

MARQUETTE

HURON

GREEN
MOUNTAIN
○ LEBANON
○ RUTLAND

WHITE
MOUNTAIN

○ AUGUSTA

ALBANY ○

○ SPRINGFIELD

○ HARTFORD

ALLEGHENY

○ TRENTON

○ HARRISBURG

WAYNE

MONONGAHELA

WASHINGTON

SHENANDOAH

GEORGE
WASHINGTON

○ ROANOKE

CUMBERLAND

JEFFERSON

CHEROKEE

PISGAH

UWHARRIE

GREAT SMOKY
MOUNTAINS

PISGAH
○ ASHEVILLE

CROATAN

CHEROKEE

NANTAHALA

CHATTAHOOCHEE

SUMTER

○ GAINESVILLE

MT OGLETHORPE

○ ATLANTA

OCONEE

FRANCIS
MARION

TALLADEGA

CHATTAHOOCHEE

TUSKEGEE

CONECUH

APALACHICOLA

OSCEOLA

OCALA

LEGEND

••••• APPALACHIAN TRAIL

▬▬▬ NATIONAL FORESTS

▬▬▬ NATIONAL PARKS

WOOD WATER FORAGE
FOREST SERVICE
US
WILDLIFE RECREATION

The Trail through Maine is roughly divided into three sections. The eastern, the 120 miles from Mt. Katahdin to Mason, is characterized by disconnected mountains and is studded with many lakes, ponds, and streams, and beautiful forest. The second portion runs from Blanchard across the Kenneboc River to twin-peaked Mt. Bigelow. The first section involves considerable climbing and exertion, but the remainder affords easier travel. The third or western portion is in an area of rough, steep 4,000-foot mountains and leads the hiker into a considerable amount of ascent and descent.

The New Hampshire Section

The White Mountain region is well known and frequently traveled. The Appalachian Trail reaches the crest of the Presidential Range at Mt. Madison and then leads past Mts. Jefferson and Clay over Mt. Washington (6,288 feet). Much of the Trail is above timberline, where the temperatures may change abruptly. The trip calls for intelligent planning and generous travel time should be allowed. The connecting link between the Green and White Mountains passes through a broken terrain, east of the Connecticut River, alternating forest-covered mountains and valleys.

The Trail Through Vermont

West of the Connecticut River to the Green Mountains, the route is through high rough country of abandoned and overgrown farms and woodlands.

Northeast of Rutland, Vermont, at Sherburne Pass, the Trail joins the Green Mountain Club's famed 225-mile "Long Trail" and follows the lower 95 miles of it along the crest of the Green Mountains. The dominating peak is Killington (4,241 feet).

Hiking Through Massachusetts

The Appalachian Trail leads through the Berkshire Hills. There are pleasant hikes through a series of wooded areas and many valleys, and climbs over such outstanding peaks as Mt. Greylock and Mt. Everett.

Going Through Connecticut

The Trail through Connecticut is a meandering route through weathered and worn remnants of a formerly much loftier mountain range. This is a scenic trail and affords much variety along the Housatonic Valley and the Taconic Range.

The New York-New Jersey Section

From the State of Connecticut to Kittatinny Range in New Jersey, the Trail is less rugged and wild. East of the Hudson River, much of the path follows old roads which, however, afford interesting hikes and a change of scene. The Trail along the Kittatinny Range is more remote and rugged than the remainder of this section.

The Pennsylvania Route

The Appalachian Trail System in Pennsylvania follows the east range of the Allegheny Mountains. Beyond the Susquehanna River, some 10 miles, it crosses the historic Cumberland Valley and follows the northernmost extension of the Blue Ridge Mountains. The Cumberland Valley crossing involves some 13 miles of hiking along roads through farmland.

Walking Through Maryland

This portion of the Trail is never too far from roads and towns, where supplies or other accommodations may be obtained. Travel time takes about three or four days. One pleasing stretch runs 38 miles along the ridge crest of South Mountain.

The Virginia Section

About one-fourth of the Appalachian Trail System lies in Virginia. Unfortunately, the northermost 50 miles is privately-owned land, where permission to travel could be revoked at any time for any misconduct. The next section lies in the Shenandoah National Park with 100 miles of excellent trail and numerous side trail trips. Views in this area are outstanding. Beyond, the Trail follows a course roughly parallel to the famous Blue Ridge Parkway, but it is many miles removed. It crosses the Parkway twice in the 70 miles in the Pedlar District of the George Washington National Forest. This section is through mature timber and wilderness terrain with

Mt. Katahdin.

high mountain summits, and it is perhaps more impressive to the backpacking traveler than the region to the north. The southern portion features beautiful stands of rhododendron and azalea with their spectacular bloom coming in the late Spring.

Tennessee-North Carolina

From Damascus, Virginia, the Trail follows segments of several mountain ranges of the Cherokee National Forest to the North Carolina-Tennessee line. As it moves on through the Pisgah National Forest the hiker is introduced to the majesty of the southern Appalachian

Mountains. The most primitive section and the highest of the entire trail passes along the crest line of the Great Smoky Mountains National Park for 70 miles. Beyond the Great Smokies one crosses the Yellow Creek-Wauchecha-Cheoah Mountain region, which is rugged and sometimes difficult to travel. Next comes the Nantahala National Forest section, with 4,000-foot gaps and 5,000-foot peaks.

Georgia — The Last Stretch!

Here the Trail passes through the beautiful Chattahoochee National Forest. The wilderness environment, elevation and ruggedness of the region are decidedly unexpected toward this southern terminus. Highways cross the Blue Ridge at intervals and the area is readily accessible.

Trail Guides

In planning a trip, Trail users need to know points of access and egress, possible shelter, sources of supplies, points of interest, and, most important, some landmarks by which to orient themselves while on the Trail, particularly in cases of emergency. To supply this information, the Appalachian Trail Conference and its member clubs have prepared nine guidebooks, covering the entire Trail. They are: Maine; New Hampshire and Vermont; Massachusetts and Connecticut; New York, New Jersey, and Pennsylvania east of the Susquehanna River; Pennsylvania west of the Susquehanna River, Maryland and Virginia north of the Shenandoah

National Park; the Shenandoah National Park; Central and Southwestern Virginia; Tennessee and North Carolina (Cherokee, Pisgah, and the Great Smokies); the Great Smokies, Nantahalas, and Georgia.

These guidebooks give all the information needed to plan a trip, indicating lean-tos in each area, as well as other accommodations if known to be available. The guides are listed, with their prices, in *The Appalachian Trail* (Publication No. 17), a booklet available from The Appalachian Trail Conference, 1718 N Street N.W., Washington, D.C. 20036. This booklet also lists other publications of interest to the hiker and backpacker, and it offers suggestions for trips, showing in which areas one can travel without a tent, relying on lean-tos; where on the Trail all camping equipment is needed; and where public accommodations (sporting camps, huts, farm and tourist houses) are accessible, permitting the hiker to carry only his personal effects.

For anyone who has never traveled the Appalachian Trail, or in fact any other trails, the Conference publishes *Suggestions for Appalachian Trail Users* (Publication No. 15). *The Appalachian Trail* (Publication No. 5) will also be helpful. And all hikers and backpackers should have a copy of *Lightweight Equipment for Hiking, Camping, and Mountaineering,* which contains names of outfitters, addresses, articles, description, weight and price. It was compiled by the Potomac Appalachian Trail Club and is available from them at 1718 N Street N.W., Washington, D.C. 20036. Prices of these publications vary from year to year, so it is best to obtain a current list before ordering. Inquirers are requested to send 25 cents to cover the cost of mailing information packets.

The Appalachian Mountain Club also offers guides, maps, and other publications covering all hiking trails of Maine, New Hampshire, and Massachusetts-Rhode Island. In addition to their own publications they handle guides from other organizations and mountain books of interest. You can write for a list to the Club at 5 Joy Street, Boston, Massachusetts 02108.

Foot Travelers Only

The use of motorized vehicles, bicycles, or horses on the Appalachian Trail is prohibited by the public authorities in most areas. Horses and vehicles cut ground cover and create erosion and ruts, resulting in heavy trail damage and difficult going for hikers. The Trail was not laid out or intended for travelers other than those on foot. Certain portions are of a standard to permit horseback travel; however, even these sections have been damaged by horseback travel.

The Horse-Shoe Trail

An extensive side trail to the Appalachian Trail in Pennsylvania has been designed expressly for horse-back travel. It is the Horse-Shoe Trail, and it extends from Valley Forge to the Appalachian Trail at Rattling Run near the Susquehanna River. This trail is marked by yellow paint blazes and horseshoes. For full information, obtain *Guide To The Horse-Shoe Trail* ($1) from the Horse-Shoe Trail Club, Inc., 1600 Three Penn Center Plaza, Philadelphia, Pennsylvania 19102.

Following Trail Markers

Keeping to the trail is the surest and safest way of arriving at your destination. Generally, forest and park trails are cleared of underbrush and well drained by water-turnouts where needed. Routes are indicated by various types of trail markers. Trail blazes are primary methods of marking trails in the western states. In some parts of the United States they consist of painted or plain vertical cuttings or slashes on the bark of a tree about 6 inches long and 2 to 4 inches wide at either eye or saddle height.

Galvanized-iron tags or plates about 4 inches square are used on the Appalachian Trail. A double blaze indi-

Youngsters heading into the White Mountains.

cates a turn in the Trail. In some sections paint marks are still used. Markers are generally placed four to the mile in each direction.

In areas where there are few trees, painted blazes may be located on conspicuous rocks and ledges at about eye level, so as not to be obliterated by the snow. A route across open fields can also be indicated by rock cairns, consisting of a number of stones or rocks built one on top of the other, pyramid style. They are generally placed 100 feet apart, so that they may be distinguishable during inclement weather. Some hikers call the rock cairn trail markers "ducks."

A trail shelter in North Carolina.

Lean-to Shelters

Along many sections of the Trail one will find a lean-to type of open-faced shelter, but there are variations in those erected along the Trail. The lean-to is designed to furnish only protection from the elements. Most of such structures have some provision for bunks. Each structure has a fireplace, usually in front. In addition, there usually is a spring nearby, garbage pit, and a latrine.

Use of the lean-to is on a first-come basis. Lean-tos also make it unnecessary to carry a tent, but all other camping equipment, including axe or stove and fuel must be brought. The hiker should realize, however, that some of the lean-tos are small, and in a much-frequented area, he may arrive late in the day only to find it occupied. This problem seldom arises except in readily accessible and well-known areas such as the Palisades Interstate, Shenandoah, and Great Smoky Mountains Parks and on the Long Trail. Solutions suggested by the Appalachian Trail Conference are to try less crowded areas, to go off-season, or to carry a lightweight plastic "fly" as insurance.

Vandalism

It is imperative that each Trail user exercise the utmost care to preserve the structures and attractive surroundings. Vandalism and carelessness in use presents many maintenance problems and in the case of privately-owned lands may mean closing of the area to the public. Above all, see that your fire is out!

APPENDIX

National Forests, Parks, Monuments, & Recreaton Areas

ALABAMA

William B. Bankhead National Forest, Box 40,
   Montgomery 36101
Conecuh National Forest, Box 40, Montgomery 36101
Horseshoe Bend National Military Park, Box 608,
   Dadeville 36853
Natchez Trace Parkway, Box 948, Tupelo, Mississippi
   (sections of parkway also located in Tennessee
   and Mississippi)
Russell Cave National Monument, Bridgeport 35740
Talladega National Forest, Box 40, Montgomery 36101
Tuskegee National Forest, Box 40, Montgomery 36101

ALASKA

Chugach National Forest, 328 E. 4th Ave.,
   Anchorage 99501
Glacier Bay National Monument, Box 1781,
   Juneau 99801
Katmai National Monument, c/o Mt. McKinley
   National Park, McKinley Park 99755
Mt. McKinley National Park, McKinley Park 99755
Sitka National Monument, Box 1781, Juneau 99801

North Tongass National Forest, 217 2nd St.,
    Juneau 99801
South Tongass National Forest, Box 2278,
    Ketchikan 99901

ARIZONA

Apache National Forest, Springerville 85938
Canyon de Chelly National Monument, Box 8,
    Chinle 86503
Casa Grande Ruins National Monument, Box 518,
    Coolidge 85228
Chiricahua National Monument, Dos Cabezas
    Star Route, Wilcox 85643
Coconino National Forest, 114 N. San Francisco St.,
    Flagstaff 86002
Coronado National Forest, Post Office Building,
    Tucson 85702
Coronado National Memorial, Star Route,
    Hereford 85615
Glen Canyon National Recreation Area, Box 1507,
    Page 86040 (part of area located in Utah)
Grand Canyon National Park, Box 129,
    Grand Canyon 86023
Grand Canyon National Monument, c/o Grand Canyon
    National Park, Box 129, Grand Canyon 86023
Kaibab National Forest, 107 N. Second St.,
    Williams 86046
Lake Mead National Recreation Area, 601 Nevada
    Highway, Boulder City, Nevada 89005
    (part of area located in Nevada)
Montezuma Castle National Monument, Box 218,
    Camp Verde 86322
Navajo National Monument, Tonalea 86044

Organ Pipe Cactus National Monument,
     Box 38, Ajo 85321
Petrified Forest National Park, Holbrook 86025
Pipe Spring National Monument,
     Springdale, Utah 84767
Prescott National Forest, 344 S. Cortez St.,
     Prescott 86301
Suguaro National Monument, Route 8, Box 350,
     Tucson 85710
Sitgreaves National Forest, 113 W. Hopi Dr.,
     Holbrook 86025
Susan Crater National Monument, c/o Wupatki
     National Monument, Tuba Star Route,
     Flagstaff 86003
Tonto National Forest, 230 N. First Ave., Room 6208,
     Phoenix 85025
Tonto National Monument, Box 1088, Roosevelt 85545
Tumacacori National Monument, Box 67,
     Tumacacori 85640
Tuzigoot National Monument, Box 36,
     Clarksdale 86324
Walnut Canyon National Monument, Route 1,
     Box 790, Flagstaff 86001
Wupatki National Monument, Tuba Star Route,
     Flagstaff 86001

ARKANSAS

Arkansas Post National Memorial, c/o Hot Springs
     National Park, Box 1219, Hot Springs 71902
Fort Smith National Historic Site, Box 1406,
     Fort Smith 72902
Hot Springs National Park, Box 1219,
     Hot Springs 71902

Ouachita National Forest, Box 1270,
    Hot Springs 71902
Ozark and St. Francis National Forests, Forest Service
    Building, Russellville 72801
Pea Ridge National Military Park, Pea Ridge 72751

CALIFORNIA

Angeles National Forest, 1015 N. Lake St.,
    Pasadena 91104
Cabrillo National Monument, Box 6175,
    San Diego 92106
Channel Islands National Monument, Box 6175,
    San Diego 92106
Cleveland National Forest, 1196 Broadway,
    San Diego 92101
Death Valley National Monument, Death Valley
    92328 (portion of area also in Nevada)
Devils Postpile National Monument, Box 577,
    Yosemite National Park 95389
Eldorado National Forest, Placerville 95667
Inyo National Forest, 207 W. South St., Bishop 93514
Joshua Tree National Monument, Box 875,
    Twentynine Palms 92277
Kings Canyon National Park, Three Rivers 93271
Klamath National Forest, Yreka 96097
Lassen National Forest, Susanville 96130
Lassen Volcanic National Park, Mineral 96063
Lava Beds National Monument, Box 867,
    Tulelake 96134
Los Padres National Forest, Federal Building,
    Santa Barbara 93101
Mendocino National Forest, Willows 95988

Modoc National Forest, Alturas 96101
Muir Woods National Monument, Mill Valley 94943
Pinnacles National Monument, Paicines 95043
Plumas National Forest, Quincy 95971
Point Reyes National Seashore, Point Reyes 94956
San Bernardino National Forest, 175 West 5th Street,
    San Bernardino 92401
Sequoia National Forest, Porterville 93258
Sequoia National Park, Three Rivers 93271
Shasta-Trinity National Forest, 1615 Continental St.,
    Redding 96001
Sierra National Forest, 4831 E. Shield Ave.,
    Fresno 93726
Six Rivers National Forest, 331 J St., Eureka 95501
Stanislaus National Forest, Sonora 95370
Tahoe National Forest, Nevada City 95959
Toiyabe National Forest, 1555 South Wells Ave.,
    Reno, Nevada 89502
Yosemite National Park, Box 577, Yosemite 95389

COLORADO

Arapaho National Forest, 1010 Tenth St.,
    Golden 80402
Bent's Old Fort National Historic Site, Box 581,
    LaJunta 81050
Black Canyon of the Gunnison National Monument,
    c/o Curecanti National Recreation Area,
    Montrose 81401
Colorado National Monument, c/o Curecanti National
    Recreation Area, Montrose 81401
Dinosaur National Monument, Artesia 81610
    (part of area located in Utah)

Grand Mesa-Uncompahgre National Forests,
    Delta 81416
Great Sand Dunes National Monument, Box 60,
    Alamosa 81101
Gunnison National Forest, Columbine Hotel,
    Gunnison 81230
Hovenweep National Monument, c/o Mesa Verde
    National Park 81330 (part of area located in Utah)
Mesa Verde National Park, Mesa Verde 81330
Pike National Forest, Post Office Building,
    Colorado Springs 80901
Rio Grande National Forest, Fassett Building,
    Monte Vista 81144
Rocky Mountain National Park, Box 1080,
    East Park 80517
Roosevelt National Forest, Post Office Building,
    Fort Collins 80522
Routt National Forest, Hunt Building, Steamboat
    Spring 80477
San Isabel National Forest, Pueblo 81002
San Juan National Forest, West Building,
    Durango 81301
Shadow Mountain National Recreation Area,
    c/o Rocky Mountain National Park,
    Box 1080, Estes Park 80517
White River National Forest, Glenwood Springs 81601

DISTRICT OF COLUMBIA

Battleground National Cemetery, National Capital
    Region, National Park Service, Washington 20242
House Where Lincoln Died National Memorial,

National Capital Region, National Park Service,
    Washington 20242
Lincoln Memorial National Memorial, National
    Capital Region, National Park Service,
    Washington 20242
Lincoln Museum National Memorial, National Capital
    Region, National Park Service, Washington 20242
National Capital Parks, National Capital Region,
    National Park Service, Washington 20242
    (also areas in Maryland and Virginia)
Pennsylvania Avenue National Historic Site,
    c/o National Capital Parks
Thomas Jefferson National Memorial, National Capital
    Region, National Park Service, Washington 20242
Washington Monument National Memorial, National
    Capital Region, National Park Service,
    Washington 20242
White House National Capital Region, National Park
    Service, Washington 20242

FLORIDA

Apalachicola National Forest, Box 1050,
    Tallahassee 32302
Castillo de San Marcos National Monument,
    1 Castillo Drive, St. Augustine 32084
De Soto National Memorial, Box 1377,
    Bradenton 33506
Everglades National Park, Box 279, Homestead 33030
Fort Caroline National Memorial, 1 Castillo Dr.,
    St. Augustine 32084
Fort Jefferson National Monument, c/o Everglades
    National Park, Box 279, Homestead 33030

Fort Matanzas National Monument, 1 Castillo Dr.,
    St. Augustine 32084
Ocala National Forest, Box 1050, Tallahassee 32302
Osceola National Forest, Box 1050, Tallahassee 32302

GEORGIA

Chattahoochee National Forest, P. O. Box 643,
    Gainesville 30501
Chickamauga and Chattanooga National Military Park,
    Fort Oglethorpe 30742 (part of park in Tennessee)
Fort Frederica National Monument, Box 816,
    St. Simons Island 31522
Fort Pulaski National Monument, Box 98,
    Savannah Beach 31328
Kennesaw Mountain National Battlefield Park,
    Box 1167, Marietta 30061
Ocmulgee National Monument, Box 4186,
    Macon 31208
Oconee National Forest, P. O. Box 643,
    Gainesville 30501

HAWAII

City of Refuge National Historical Park, Honaunau,
    Kona, Hawii 96726
Haleakala National Park, Box 456, Kahului,
    Maui 96732
Hawaii Volcanoes National Park, Hawaii 96718

IDAHO

Boise National Forest, 210 Main St., Boise 83702
Caribou National Forest, 427 North Sixth Ave.,
    Pocatello 83201

Challis National Forest, Challis 83226
Clearwater National Forest, Orofino 83544
Coeur d'Alene National Forest, Coeur d'Alene 83814
Craters of the Moon National Monument, Box 29,
    Arco 83213
Kaniksu National Forest, Sandpoint 83864
Kootenai National Forest, Libby, Montana 59923
Nezperce National Forest, Grangeville 83530
Payette National Forest, McCall 83638
Salmon National Forest, Salmon 83467
Sawtooth National Forest, 1525 Addison Avenue East,
    Twin Falls 83301
St. Joe National Forest, St. Maries 83861
Targhee National Forest, St. Anthony 83445
Yellowstone National Park, Yellowstone Park,
    Wyoming 83020 (sections of park also in
    Wyoming and Montana)

ILLINOIS

Chicago Portage National Historic Site (not owned
    by the Federal Government), Superintendent,
    Cook County Forest Preserve, Cummings
    Square, River Forest
Shawnee National Forest, Harrisburg National Bank
    Building, Harrisburg 62946

INDIANA

Hoosier National Forest, Stone City National Bank
    Building, Bedford 47421
Lincoln Boyhood National Memorial,
    Lincoln City 47552

IOWA

Effigy Mounds, National Monument, Box K,
    McGregor 52157
Herbert Hoover National Historic Site, West Branch

KENTUCKY

Abraham Lincoln Birthplace National Historic Site,
    Route 1, Hodgenville 42748
Cumberland National Forest, Winchester 40391
Cumberland Gap National Historical Park, Box 840,
    Middlesboro 40965 (sections of park also in
    Tennessee and Virginia)
Mammoth Cave National Park, Mammoth Cave 42259

LOUISIANA

Chalmette National Historical Park, Box 125,
    Arabi 70032
Kisatchie National Forest, Box 471, Alexandria 71302

MAINE

Acadia National Park, Box 338, Bar Harbor 04609
White Mountain National Forest, Federal Building,
    Laconia, New Hampshire 03246

MARYLAND

Antietam National Battlefield Site, Box 158,
    Sharpsburg 21782
Antietam National Cemetery, Box 158,
    Sharpsburg 21782

Chesapeake and Ohio Canal National Monument,
    479 North Potomac Street, Hagerstown 21740
    (portion of area in West Virginia)
Fort McHenry National Monument and Historic
    Shrine, Baltimore 21230
George Washington Memorial Parkway, c/o National
    Capital Region, National Park Service,
    Washington, D. C. 20242 (section of parkway
    in Virginia)
Hampton National Historic Site, c/o Fort McHenry
    National Monument, Baltimore 21230
Harpers Ferry National Historical Park, Box 117,
Harpers Ferry, West Virginia 25425
    (portion of area in West Virginia)
National Capital Parks, c/o National Capital Region,
    National Park Service, Washington, D. C. 20242
    (also areas in District of Columbia, Virginia and
    West Virginia)

MASSACHUSETTS

Adams National Historic Site, 135 Adams St.,
    Quincy 02169
Cape Code National Seashore, Box 428,
    Eastham 02642
Dorchester Heights National Historic Site (not owned
    by the Federal Government), c/o Department
    of Parks, Boston
Minute Man National Historical Park, Room 1400
    Post Office and Courthouse Building,
    Boston 02109
Salem Maritime National Historic Site, Custom House,
    Derby St., Salem 01970

MICHIGAN

Hiawatha National Forest, Escanaba 49829
Huron National Forest, Cadillac 49601
Isle Royale National Park, 87 N. Ripley St.,
　　Houghton 49931
Manistee National Forest, Cadillac 49601
Ottawa National Forest, Ironwood 49938

MINNESOTA

Chippewa National Forest, Cass Lake 56633
Grand Portage National Monument, Box 666,
　　Grand Marais 55604
Pipestone National Monument, Box 727,
　　Pipestone 56164
Superior National Forest, Federal Building,
　　Duluth 55801

MISSISSIPPI

Bienville National Forest, Box 1291, Jackson 39205
Brices Cross Roads National Battlefield Site, c/o
　　Natchez Trace Parkway, Box 948, Tupelo 38802
Delta National Forest, Box 1291, Jackson 39205
De Soto National Forest, Box 1291, Jackson 39205
Holly Springs National Forest, Box 1291,
　　Jackson 39205
Homochitto National Forest, Box 1291, Jackson 39205
Natchez Trace Parkway, Box 948, Tupelo (portions
　　of parkway also in Alabama and Tennessee)
Tombigbee National Forest, Box 1291, Jackson 39205
Tupelo National Battlefield, c/o Natchez Trace
　　Parkway, Box 948, Tupelo 38802

Vicksburg National Cemetery, Box 349,
    Vicksburg 39181
Vicksburg National Military Park, Box 349,
    Vicksburg 39181

MISSOURI

Clark National Forest, Rolla 65401
George Washington Carver National Monument,
    Box 38, Diamond 64840
Jefferson National Expansion Memorial National
    Historic Site, 11 N. 4th St., St. Louis 63102
Mark Twain National Forest, Springfield 65806
Wilson's Creek National Battlefield Park, c/o George
    Washington Carver National Monument

MONTANA

Beaverhead National Forest, Dillon 59725
Big Hole National Battlefield, c/o Yellowstone
    National Park, Wyoming 83020
Bitterroot National Forest, Hamilton 59840
Custer National Forest, Billings 59101
Custer Battlefield National Monument, Box 116,
    Crow Agency 59022
Deerlodge National Forest, Butte 59701
Flathead National Forest, Kalispell 59901
Gallatin National Forest, Bozeman 59715
Glacier National Park, West Glacier 59936
Helena National Forest, Helena 59601
Kootenai National Forest, Libby 59923
Lewis and Clark National Forest, Great Falls 59401
Lolo National Forest, Missoula 59801

Yellowstone National Park, Yellowstone Park,
    Wyoming 83020 (portions of park in Wyoming
    and Idaho)

NEBRASKA

Chimney Rock National Historic Site (not owned by
    Federal Government), c/o Superintendent,
    Scotts Bluff National Monument, Box 427,
    Gering 69341
Homestead National Monument of America,
    Beatrice 68310
Nebraska National Forest, Post Office Building,
    Lincoln 68508
Scotts Bluff National Monument, Box 427,
    Gering 69341

NEVADA

Death Valley National Monument, Death Valley,
    California 92328 (portion of area in California)
Humboldt National Forest, Post Office Building,
    Elko 89901
Lake Mead National Recreation Area, 601 Nevada
    Highway, Boulder City 89005 (portion of area
    in Arizona)
Lehman Caves National Monument, Baker 89311
Toiyabe National Forest, 1555 South Wells Avenue,
    Reno 89502

NEW HAMPSHIRE

White Mountain National Forest, Federal Building,
    Laconia 03246

NEW JERSEY

Edison National Historic Site, Box 126, Orange 07051
Morristown National Historical Park, Box 759,
    Morristown 07960

NEW MEXICO

Aztec Ruins National Monument, Route 1, Box 101,
    Aztec 87410
Bandelier National Monument, Los Alamos 87544
Capulin Mountain National Monument, Box 94,
    Capulin 88414
Carlsbad Caverns National Park, Box 1598,
    Carlsbad 88220
Carson National Forest, Taos 87571
Chaco Canyon National Monument, Box 156,
    Bloomfield 87413
Cibola National Forest, 304 U. S. Courthouse,
    Albuquerque 87103
Coronado National Forest, Tucson, Arizona 85702
El Morro National Monument, Ramah 87321
Fort Union National Monument, Watrous 87753
Gila National Forest, 301 West College Avenue,
    Silver City 88061
Gila Cliff Dwellings National Monument, Box 1320,
    Silver City 88061
Gran Quivira National Monument, Route 1,
    Mountainair 87036
Lincoln National Forest, Alamogordo 88310
Santa Fe National Forest, 130 Capitol Pl.,
    Santa Fe 87501
White Sands National Monument, Box 458,
    Alamogordo 88310

NEW YORK

Castle Clinton National Monument, c/o New York
City National Park Service Group, 28 East
20th St., New York 10003

Federal Hall National Memorial, c/o New York City
National Park Service Group, 28 East
20th St., New York 10003

Fire Island National Seashore, P. O. Box 229,
Patchogue, Long Island 11773

General Grant National Memorial, c/o New York
City National Park Service Group, 28 East
20th St., New York 10003

Home of Franklin D. Roosevelt National Historic Site,
Hyde Park, Dutchess County 12538

St. Paul's Church National Historic Site (not owned
by Federal Government), Rector, Corporation
of St. Paul's Church, 859 S. Columbus Ave.,
Mount Vernon 10550

Sagamore Hill National Historic Site, Oyster Bay,
Long Island 11771

Saratoga National Historical Park, Route 1, Box 113-C,
Stillwater 12170

Statue of Liberty National Monument, c/o New York
City National Park Service Group, 28 East 20th
Street, New York 10003

Theodore Roosevelt Birthplace National Historic Site,
c/o New York City National Park Service Group,
28 East 20th St., New York 10003

Vanderbilt Manison National Historic Site, Hyde Park,
Dutchess County 12538

NORTH CAROLINA

Blue Ridge Parkway, Box 1710, Roanoke,

Virginia 24008 (portion of parkway also
in Virginia)

Cape Hatteras National Seashore, Box 457,
Manteo 27954

Croatan National Forest, Box 731, Asheville 28802

Fort Raleigh National Historic Site, Box 457,
Manteo 27954

Great Smoky Mountains National Park, Gatlinburg,
Tennessee 37738 (portion of area in Tennessee)

Guilford Courthouse National Military Park, Box 9145,
Plaza Station, Greensboro 27408

Moores Creek National Military Park, Currie,
Pender County 28435

Nantahala National Forest, Box 731, Ashville 28802

Pisgah National Forest, Box 731, Asheville 28802

Uwharrie National Forest, Box 731, Asheville 28802

Wright Brothers National Memorial, Box 457,
Manteo 27954

NORTH DAKOTA

Theodore Roosevelt National Memorial Park,
Medora 58645

OHIO

Mound City Group National Monument, Box 327,
Chillicothe 45601

Perry's Victory and International Peace Memorial
National Monument, Box 78, Put-in-Bay 43456

Wayne National Forest, Stone City National Bank
Building, Bedford, Indiana 47421

OKLAHOMA

Ouachita National Forest, Box 1270, Hot Springs,
    Arkansas 71902
Platt National Park, Box 379, Sulphur 73086

OREGON

Crater Lake National Park, Box 7, Crater Lake 97604
Deschutes National Forest, Bend 97701
Fort Clatsop National Memorial, Box 604 FC,
    Astoria 97103
Fremont National Forest, Lakeview 97630
Malheur National Forest, Grant County Bank Building,
    John Day 97845
McLoughlin House National Historic Site (not owned
    by Federal Government), Curator,
    Oregon City 97045
Mt. Hood National Forest, P. O. Box 5241,
    Portland 97216
Ochoco National Forest, Bottero Building,
    Prineville 97754
Oregon Caves National Monument, Box 7,
    Crater Lake 97604
Rogue River National Forest, Medford 97501
Siskiyou National Forest, Grants Pass 97526
Siuslaw National Forest, Ash Building, Corvallis 97330
Umatilla National Forest, Pendleton 97801
Umpqua National Forest, Federal Office Building,
    Roseburg 97470
Wallowa-Whitman National Forests, Baker 97814
Willamette National Forest, Post Office Building,
    Eugene 97401
Winema National Forest, Klamath Falls 97601

PENNSYLVANIA

Allegheny National Forest, Warren 16365
Fort Necessity National Battlefield, Star Route, Box 15,
    Farmington 15437
Gettysburg National Cemetery, Gettysburg 17325
Gettysburg National Military Park, Gettysburg 17325
Gloria Dei (Old Swedes') Church National Historic Site
    (not owned by Federal Government), Rector,
    Delaware Avenue and Christian Street,
    Philadelphia
Hopewell Village National Historic Site, Route 1,
    Elverson 19520
Independence National Historical Park,
    420 Chestnut St., Philadelphia 19106

RHODE ISLAND

Touro Synogogue National Historic Site (not owned
    by Federal Government), President, The Society
    of Friends of Touro Synogogue National Historic
    Shrine, Inc., 85 Touro St., Newport 02840

SOUTH CAROLINA

Cowpens National Battlefield Site, c/o Kings Mountain
    National Military Park, Box 31, Kings Mountain,
    North Carolina 28086
Fort Sumter National Monument, Box 428,
    Sullivan's Island 29482
Francis Marion National Forest, 901 Sumter St.,
    Columbia 29201
Kings Mountain National Military Park, Box 31,
    Kings Mountain, North Carolina 28086

Sumter National Forest, 901 Sumter St.,
    Columbia 29201

SOUTH DAKOTA

Badlands National Monument, Box 72, Interior 57750
Black Hills National Forest, Custer 57730
Jewel Cave National Monument, c/o Wind Cave
    National Park, Hot Springs 57747
Mount Rushmore National Memorial, Keystone 57751
Wind Cave National Park, Hot Springs 57747

TENNESSEE

Andrew Johnson National Historic Site,
    Greenville 37743
Cherokee National Forest, P. O. Box 400,
    Cleveland 37312
Chickamauga and Chattanooga National Military Park,
    Fort Oglethorpe, Georgia 30742 (portion
    of area in Georgia)
Cumberland Gap National Historical Park, Box 840,
    Middlesboro, Kentucky 40965 (portions of area
    in Kentucky and Virginia)
Fort Donelson National Military Park, Box F,
    Dover 37058
Fort Donelson National Cemetery, Box F, Dover 37058
Great Smoky Mountains National Park, Gatlinburg
    37738 (portion of area in North Carolina)
Natchez Trace Parkway, Box 948, Tupelo, Mississippi
    (parkway also located in Alabama and Mississippi)
Shiloh National Cemetery, Shiloh 38376
Shiloh National Military Park, Shiloh 38376

Stones River National Battlefield, Box 1039,
    Murfreesboro 37131
Stones River National Cemetery, Box 1039,
    Murfreesboro 37131

TEXAS

Angelina National Forest, Box 380, Lufkin 75902
Big Bend National Park, Big Bend 79834
Davy Crockett National Forest, Box 380, Lufkin 75902
Fort Davis National Historic Site, Box 785,
    Fort Davis 70734
Padre Island National Seashore, P. O. Box 4012,
    Corpus Christi 78408
Sabine National Forest, Box 380, Lufkin 75902
Sam Houston National Forest, Box 380, Lufkin 75902
San Jose Mission National Historic Site (not owned
    by Federal Government), Manager, San Jose
    Mission National Historic Site, 6519 San Jose Dr.,
    San Antonio 78214

UTAH

Arches National Monument, c/o Canyonlands
    National Park, Uranium Bldg., Moab 84532
Ashley National Forest, Vernal 84078
Bryce Canyon National Park, Bryce Canyon 84717
Cache National Forest, Post Office Building,
    Logan 84321
Canyonlands National Park, Uranium Bldg., Moab,
    Utah 84532
Capitol Reef National Monument, Torrey 84775
Caribou National Forest, 427 North Sixth Ave.,
    Pocatello, Idaho 83201

Cedar Breaks National Monument, c/o Zion National
   Park, Springdale 84767
Dinosaur National Monument, Artesia, Colo. 81610
   (portion of area in Colorado)
Dixie National Forest, Cedar City 84720
Fishlake National Forest, Richfield 84701
Glen Canyon National Recreation Area, Box 1507,
   Page, Arizona 86040 (portion of area in Arizona)
Golden Spike National Historic Site (not owned by
   Federal Government), President, Golden Spike
   Association of Box Elder County, Brigham City,
   Utah 84302
Hovenweep National Monument, c/o Mesa Verde
   National Park, Colorado 81330 (portion of
   monument in Colorado)
Manti-La Sal National Forest, 350 East Main St.,
   Price 84501
Natural Bridges National Monument, c/o Arches
   National Monument, Box 98, Moab 84532
Rainbow Bridge National Monument, c/o Navajo
   National Monument, Tonalea, Arizona 86044
Timpanogos Cave National Monument, Route 1,
   Box 200, American Fork 84003
Uinta National Forest, Provo 84601
Wasatch National Forest, 430 South 4th St. East,
   Salt Lake City 84111
Zion National Park, Springdale 84767

VERMONT

Green Mountain National Forest, 22 Evelyn St.,
   Rutland 05701

VIRGINIA

Appomattox Court House National Historical Park,
    Box 218, Appomattox 24522
Blue Ridge Parkway, Box 1710, Roanoke 24008
    (Portion of area in North Carolina)
Booker T. Washington National Monument, Route 1,
    Box 194, Hardy 24101
Colonial National Historical Park, Box 210,
    Yorktown 23490
Cumberland Gap National Historical Park, Box 840,
    Middlesboro, Kentucky 40965 (portions of area
    in Tennessee and Kentucky)
Custis-Lee Mansion National Memorial, c/o National
    Capital Region, National Park Service,
    Washington, D. C. 20242
Fredericksburg National Cemetery, Box 679,
    Fredericksburg 22401
Fredericksburg and Spotsylvania County Battlefields
    Memorial National Military Park, Box 679,
    Fredericksburg 22401
George Washington Birthplace National Monument,
    Washington's Birthplace 22575
George Washington Memorial Parkway, c/o National
    Capital Region, National Park Service,
    Washington D. C. 20242 (section of parkway
    in Maryland)
George Washington National Forest,
    Harrisonburg 22801
Jamestown National Historic Site (not owned by
    Federal Government), Association for
    Preservation of Virginia Antiquities, John
    Marshall House, 9th and Marshall Sts.,
    Richmond 23219

Jefferson National Forest, 920 S. Jefferson St.,
    Roanoke 24001
Manassas National Battlefield Park, Manassas 22110
National Capital Parks, c/o National Capital Region,
    National Park Service, Washington 20242
    (areas also in District of Columbia and Maryland)
Petersburg National Battlefield, Box 549,
    Petersburg 23804
Poplar Grove (Petersburg) National Cemetery,
    c/o Petersburg National Battlefield, Box 549,
    Petersburg 23804
Richmond National Battlefield Park, 3215 E. Broad St.,
    Richmond 23223
Shenandoah National Park, Luray 22835
Yorktown National Cemetery, c/o Colonial National
    Historical Park, Box 210, Yorktown 23490

WASHINGTON

Colville National Forest, Colville 99114
Coulee Dam National Recreation Area, Box 37,
    Coulee Dam 99116
Fort Vancouver National Historic Site,
    Vancouver 98661
Gifford Pinchot National Forest, 1408 Franklin St.,
    Vancouver, 98661
Mount Baker National Forest, Bellingham 98225
Mount Rainier National Park, Longmire 98397
Okanogan National Forest, Okanogan 98840
Olympic National Forest, Post Office Building,
    Olympia 98501
Olympic National Park, 600 E. Park Ave.,
    Port Angeles, 98362

Snoqualmie National Forest, 905 Second Ave. Building,
    Seattle 98104
Wenatchee National Forest, Wenatchee 98801
Whitman Mission National Historic Site, Route 2,
    Walla Walla 99362

WEST VIRGINIA

Chesapeake and Ohio Canal National Monument,
    479 North Potomac St., Hagerstown 21740
    (portion of area in Maryland)
Harpers Ferry National Historical Park, Box 117,
    Harpers Ferry 25425 (portion of area
    in Maryland)
Monongahela National Forest, Federal Building,
    Elkins 26241

WISCONSIN

Chequamegon National Forest, Park Falls 54552
Nicolet National Forest, Merchants State Bank
    Building, Rhinelander 54501

WYOMING

Bighorn National Forest, Columbus Building,
    Sheridan 82801
Black Hills National Forest, Custer,
    South Dakota 55730
Bridger National Forest, Kemmerer 83101
Caribou National Forest, 427 North Sixth Ave.,
    Pocatello, Idaho 83201
Devils Tower National Monument, Devils Tower 82714

Fort Laramie National Historic Site,
    Fort Laramie 82212
Grand Teton National Park, Box 67, Moose 83012
Medicine Bow National Forest, Laramie 82071
Shoshone National Forest, Blair Office Building No. 1,
    Cody 82414
Teton National Forest, Jackson 73001
Yellowstone National Park, Yellowstone Park 83020
    (portions of park in Idaho and Montana)

PUERTO RICO

Caribbean National Forest, Box 577, Rio Piedras 00928
San Juan National Historic Site, Box 712,
    San Juan 00902

VIRGIN ISLANDS

Buck Island Reef National Monument, c/o Virgin
    Islands National Park, Box 1707, Charlotte
    Amalie, St. Thomas 00802
Christiansted National Historic Site, c/o Virgin Islands
    National Park, Box 1707, Charlotte Amalie,
    St. Thomas 00802
St. Thomas National Historic Site, c/o Virgin Islands
    National Park, Box 1707, Charlotte Amalie,
    St. Thomas 00802
Virgin Islands National Park, Box 1707,
    Charlotte Amalie, St. Thomas 00802

NATIONAL FOREST REGIONAL

HEADQUARTERS OFFICES

(Each offers a free booklet about recreational areas in
that region)

Northern Region, Federal Building, Missoula,
Montana 59801

Rocky Mountain Region, Denver Federal Center,
Building 85, Denver, Colorado 80225

Southwestern Region, Federal Building, Albuquerque,
New Mexico 87101

Intermountain Region, Forest Service Building, Ogden,
Utah 84403

California Region, 630 Sansome St., San Francisco,
California 94111

Pacific Northwest Region, P. O. Box 3623, Portland,
Oregon 97212

Eastern Region, 6816 Market St., Upper Darby,
Pennsylvania 19082

Southern Region, 50 Seventh St., N.E., Atlanta,
Georgia 30323

North Central Region, 710 N. 6th St., Milwaukee,
Wisconsin 53203

Alaska Region, Fifth St. Office Building, Juneau,
Alaska 99801

NATIONAL PARK SERVICE

REGIONAL OFFICES

(Subject to supply and demand, individual requests for free booklets about areas in each Region will be honored by the Region in which the areas are located)

Southeast Regional Office, National Park Service,
        Federal Building, Box 10008, Richmond,
        Virginia 23240

Midwest Regional Office, National Park Service,
        1709 Jackson St., Omaha, Nebraska 68102

Southwest Regional Office, National Park Service,
        Box 728, Santa Fe, New Mexico 87501

Western Regional Office, National Park Service,
        450 Golden Gate Ave., San Francisco,
        California 94105

Northeast Regional Office, National Park Service,
        143 South Third St., Philadelphia,
        Pennsylvania 19106

Northwest Regional Office, National Park Service,
        1424 Fourth Ave,
        Seattle, Washington 98101

National Capital Regional Office, National Park Service,
        1100 Ohio Dr., S.W., Washington, D. C. 20242

Address of the main office of the National Park Service:
        National Park Service
        Department of the Interior Building
        Washington, D. C. 20240

Wilderness-Type Areas in the
National Forests

State and Area	National Forest	Headquarters	Total Acreage
ARIZONA			
Blue Range (also in N. Mex.)	Apache	Springerville	216,737
Chiricahua	Coronado	Tucson	18,000
Galiuro	Coronado	Tucson	55,000
Mazatzal	Tonto	Phoenix	205,000
Mount Baldy	Apache	Springerville	7,400
Pine Mountain	Prescott	Prescott	17,445
	Tonto	Phoenix	
Sierra Ancha	Tonto	Phoenix	20,850
Superstition	Tonto	Phoenix	124,140
Sycamore Canyon	Coconino	Flagstaff	45,952
	Kaibab	Williams	
	Prescott	Prescott	
CALIFORNIA			
Agua Tibia	Cleveland	San Diego	25,995
Caribou	Lassen	Susanville	19,080
Cucamonga	San Bernardino	San Bernardino	9,022
Desolation Valley	Eldorado	Placerville	41,343
Devil Canyon-Bear Canyon	Angeles	Pasadena	35,267
Emigrant Basin	Stanislous	Sonora	97,020
High Sierra	Inyo	Bishop	393,899
	Sierra	Fresno	
	Sequoia	Porterville	
Hoover	Toiyabe	Reno, Nev.	42,800
	Inyo	Bishop, Calif.	
Marble Mountain	Klamath	Yreka	213,283
Mt. Dana-Minerals	Inyo	Bishop	82,181
	Sierra	Fresno	
Salmon Trinity Alps	Klamath	Yreka	223,300
	Shasta-Trinity	Redding	
San Gorgonio	San Bernardino	San Bernardino	33,898
San Jacinto	San Bernardino	San Bernardino	20,565
San Rafael	Los Padres	Santa Barbara	74,160
South Warner	Modoc	Alturas	68,870
Thousand Lakes	Lassen	Susanville	15,695
Ventana	Los Padres	Santa Barbara	52,129
Yolla Bolly-Middle Eel	Mendocino	Willows	109,315
	Shasta-Trinity	Redding	
COLORADO			
Flat Tops	White River	Glenwood Springs	117,800
Gore Range-Eagle Nest	Arapaho	Golden	61,204
	White River	Glenwood Springs	
La Garita	Gunnison	Gunnison	49,000
	Rio Grande	Monte Vista	
Maroon Bells-Snowmass	White River	Glenwood Springs	66,100
Mt. Zirkel-Dome Peak	Routt	Steamboat Springs	53,400
Rawah	Roosevelt	Fort Collins	25,579
San Juan	San Juan	Durango	238,080
Uncompahgre	Uncompahgre	Delta	53,252
Upper Rio Grande	Rio Grande	Monte Vista	56,600
West Elk	Gunnison	Gunnison	62,000
Wilson Mountains	San Juan	Durango	27,347
	Uncompahgre	Delta	
IDAHO			
Idaho	Boise	Boise	1,224,576
	Challis	Challis	
	Salmon	Salmon	
	Payette	McCall	
Sawtooth	Boise	Boise	200,942
	Challis	Challis	
	Sawtooth	Twin Falls	
Salmon River Breaks	Nezperce	Grangeville	216,870
	Bitterroot	Hamilton, Mont.	

State and Area	National Forest	Headquarters	Total Acreage
MONTANA			
Selway-Bitterroot (see also Montana)	Clearwater	Orofino	1,239,840
	Nezperce	Grangeville	
	Lolo	Missoula, Mont.	
	Bitterroot	Hamilton, Mont.	
MINNESOTA			
Boundary Waters Canoe Area	Superior	Duluth	886,673
Absaroka	Gallatin	Bozeman	64,000
Anaconda-Pintlar	Beaverhead	Dillon	157,803
	Bitterroot	Hamilton	
	Deerlodge	Butte	
Beartooth	Gallatin	Bozeman	230,000
	Custer	Billings	
Bob Marshall	Flathead	Kalispell	950,000
	Lewis & Clark	Great Falls	
Cabinet Mountains	Kootenai	Libby	89,900
	Kaniksu	Sandpoint, Idaho	
Gates of the Mountains	Helena	Helena	28,562
Mission Mountains	Flathead	Kalispell	73,340
Selway-Bitterroot (see also Idaho)	Bitterroot	Hamilton	1,239,840
Spanish Peaks	Gallatin	Bozeman	49,800
NEVADA			
Jarbidge	Humboldt	Elko	64,667
NEW HAMPSHIRE			
Great Gulf	White Mountain	Laconia	5,400
NEW MEXICO			
Black Range	Gila	Silver City	169,196
Blue Range (see also Arizona)	Apache	Springerville, Ariz.	216,737
Gila	Gila	Silver City	567,990
Pecos	Santa Fe	Santa Fe	165,000
	Carson	Taos	
San Pedro Parks	Santa Fe	Santa Fe	41,132
Wheeler Peak	Carson	Taos	6,051
White Mountain	Lincoln	Alamogordo	28,118
NORTH CAROLINA			
Linville Gorge	Pisgah	Asheville	7,655
OREGON			
Diamond Peak	Deschutes	Bend	35,440
Eagle Cap	Wallowa-Whitman	Baker	216,250
Gearhart Mountain	Fremont	Lakeview	18,709
Kalmiopsis	Siskiyou	Grants Pass	78,850
Mt. Hood	Mt. Hood	Portland	14,160
Mt. Jefferson	Deschutes	Bend	86,700
	Mt. Hood	Portland	
Mount Washington	Deschutes	Bend	46,655
	Willamette	Eugene	
Mountain Lakes	Rogue River	Medford	23,071
Strawberry Mountain	Malheur	John Day	33,004
Three Sisters	Deschutes	Bend	749,547
UTAH			
High Uintas	Ashley	Vernal	240,717
	Wasatch	Salt Lake City	
WASHINGTON			
Glacier Peak	Mt. Baker	Bellingham	458,105
	Wenatchee	Wenatchee	
Goat Rocks	Gifford Pinchot	Vancouver	82,680
	Snoqualmie	Seattle	
Mount Adams	Gifford Pinchot	Vancouver	42,411
North Cascade	Okanogan	Okanogan	801,000
	Mt. Baker	Bellingham	
WYOMING			
Bridger	Bridger	Kemmerer	383,300
Cloud Peak	Bighorn	Sheridan	136,880
Glacier	Shoshone	Cody	177,000
North Absaroka	Shoshone	Cody	359,700
Popo Agie	Shoshone	Cody	70,000
South Absaroka	Shoshone	Cody	505,552
Stratified	Shoshone	Cody	202,000
Teton	Teton	Jackson	563,460

Bureau of Land Management Recreation Areas

☆ The Federal Recreation Permit will be required at some Bureau of Land Management campgrounds. A star beside the campground name indicates the area has been selected or is being considered for recreation fees. Some other campgrounds not marked with a star may be added to the list of those where permits are required.

ALASKA

BEDROCK CREEK CAMPGROUND. El. 1500 ft. Fishing stream, hunting, scenery; 9 mi. southwest of Central via the Steese Highway; 5 camping units with trailer space; boil water before use; June-Sept.

BRUSHKANA CAMPGROUND. El 2550 ft. Stream and mountains, fishing, hunting; 104 mi. west of Paxson via the Denali Highway; 12 camping units with trailer space; boil water before use; July-Sept.

BYER LAKE CAMPGROUND. El. 816 ft. Wilderness lake and mountain; inaccessible by highway at present — can be reached by float-plane only; 120 mi. north of Anchorage; fishing, hunting, camping, hiking; rockhounding; scenery; 1 camp unit, sanitary facilities; boil water before use; July-Sept.

CLEARWATER CAMPGROUND. El. 3000 ft. Mountainous area, fishing, hunting, camping, scenery; 56 mi. west of Paxson via the Denali Highway; 6 camping units with two trailer space accommodations; water available — boil before use; July-Sept.

☆ DELTA CAMPGROUND. El. 1200 ft. Roadside campground 1 mi. north of Delta Junction; hunting, hiking, scenery, buffalo herds; 6 camping units with trailer space; well water; May-Sept.

DENALI CAMPGROUND. El. 2800 ft. Lake and mountain area 22 mi. west of Paxson via the Denali Highway; fishing, hunting, camping, boating, scenery; 12 camping units with trailer space; boil water before use; July-Sept.

EAGLE CAMPGROUND. El. 800 ft. Historical site 1 mi. west of Eagle City; hunting, fishing, boating, scenery; 10 camping units with trailer space; spring and stream water; June-Sept.

☆ EKLUTNA LAKE RECREATION AREA. El. 868 ft. In mountains 30 mi. north of Anchorage via Glenn Highway; hunting, camping, scenery; hiking; rockhounding; geologic formations; trail riding; 30 camping units with 14 trailer space accommodations; water available — boil before use; May-Oct.

☆ FINGER LAKE CAMPGROUND. El. 340 ft., 56 mi. north of Anchorage on Glenn Highway, 5 mi. northwest of Palmer; fishing, water sports, camping, boating, swimming; 14 camping units with 5 trailer space accommodations; well water; May-Oct.

KETCHUM CREEK CAMPGROUND. El. 900 ft. Fishing stream 2 mi. west of Circle Hot Springs via the Steese Highway; hunting, camping; swimming, scenery; 8 camping units with trailer space; boil water before use; June-Sept.

LAKE LOUISE CAMPGROUND. El. 2400 ft., 20 mi. northwest of Mile 159 of Glenn Highway via the

Lake Louise Road; fishing, hunting, camping, boating, scenery; 3 camping units with trailer space; boil water before use; June-Oct.

LIBERTY CREEK. El. 2000 ft. Fishing stream, hunting, camping, scenery; Milepost 132 on Taylor Highway; 6 camping units with trailer space; boil water before use; June-Sept.

MANKOMEN LAKE RECREATION AREA. El. 3000 ft. Wilderness lake and mountain area; 180 mi. southwest of Fairbanks, 25 mi. east of Paxson Lake. Reached by air only; fishing, hunting, camping, boating, hiking, rockhounding, scenery; 10 camping units; no trailer space; water available — boil before use; July-Sept.

SALMON LAKE. El. 442 ft., 38 mi. north of Nome; hunting, fishing, camping, scenery; 4 camping units; no trailer space; boil water before use; July-Sept.

TANGLE LAKE CAMPGROUND. El. 2791 ft., 21 mi. west of Paxson via the Denali Highway; fishing, hunting, camping, boating, rockhounding; scenery; 5 camping units with 2 trailer space accommodations; water available — boil before use; July-Sept.

TANGLE RIVER CAMPGROUND. El. 2848 ft. Lake, stream and mountain area, 22 mi. west of Paxson via the Denali Highway; fishing, hunting, camping, scenery; 11 camping units with 4 trailer space accommodations; water available — boil before use; July-Sept.

TOLOVANA RIVER. El. 700 ft. Fishing stream 12 mi. southeast of Linvengood via the Elliott Highway; hunting, camping, scenery; 6 camping units with trailer space; boil water before use; June-Sept.

WALKER FORK. El. 1750 ft. Fishing stream, Mile-post 82 on Taylor Highway; hunting, camping, geologic formations, scenery; 6 camping units with trailer space; boil water before use; June-Sept.

ARIZONA

☆ HUALAPI MT. COMPLEX, WILD COW SPRINGS. El. 7500 ft. In mountains 12 mi. south of Kingman on unsurfaced Hualapi Mt. Road; scenery, hunting, hiking, rockhounding; 12 camping units; no trailer space; boil water before use; May-Nov.

CALIFORNIA

CINDER CONE. El. 3500 ft. Plateau 6 mi. southeast of Fall River Mills off U.S. 299; hunting; 13 camping units; no trailer space; boil water before use; May-Oct.

COPCO RESERVOIR. El. 2500 ft. On Klamath River 33 mi. northeast of Yreka (U.S. 99) N. Central Valley; water sports, boat launching ramp, fishing, hunting, 3 picnic sites; no trailer space; water available; cooperative area, BLM-Pacific Power and Light Company; May-Nov.

COW MOUNTAIN RECREATION AREA. El. to 2500 ft. Mountainous terrain, hunting, hiking, no trailer space, May-Oct. MAYACMAS. Off U.S. 101 9 mi. east of Ukiah on Talmage Road at McClure Creek; 7 camping units; water. SHELDON CREEK. Off U.S. 101 12 mi. east of Hopland on Highland Springs Road; 10 camping units; water. SOUTH RED MOUNTAIN. Off U.S. 101 11 mi. east of

Ukiah on New Cow Mt. Road; 12 camping units; boil water before use.

☆ DOUGLAS CITY. El. 1600 ft. Mountainous area 45 mi. west of Redding, 1 mi. west of Douglas City on paved county road off U.S. 299 on Trinity River; swimming, fishing, hunting, picnicking; 16 camping units with 20 trailer space accommodations; water. May-Nov.

☆ EAGLE LAKE. El. 5100 ft. Volcanic formation, 33 mi. north of Susanville via State Highway 139; swimming, fishing, boating, hunting; 17 camping units with 10 trailer space accommodations; water; June-Oct.

JUNCTION CITY. El. 1500 ft. On Trinity River, 10½ mi. west of Weaverville, 1½ mi. from Junction City on U.S. 299; swimming, hunting, fishing; 10 camping units; no trailer space; water; May-Oct.

KING RANGE RECREATION AREA. El. 2200 ft. Coastal mountains and beach (at low tide) beside Pacific Ocean; peaks at 4081 ft. elevation. Follow Shelter Cove Road 20 mi. west of Redway off U.S. 101. Road narrow, not recommended for trailers. Hunting, hiking, fishing, beach combing; water; May-Sept. ☆ HORSE MT. 6 mi. north of Shelter Cove Road; 9 camping units; no trailers; water. ☆ NADELOS. 2 mi. south of Shelter Cove Road; 4 mi. to beach; 4 camping units; no trailer space; water. ☆ TOLKAN. 3½ mi. north of Shelter Cove Road; 9 camping units; no trailers; boil water before use. ☆ WAILAKI. 2½ mi. south of Shelter Cove Road; 9 camping units; no trailers; water.

LAMONT MEADOWS-LONG VALLEY RECREA-
TION AREA. El. to 9000 ft. Mountain valley in
lower Sierra-Nevada Mts. From U.S. 395 turn west
7 mi. south of Little Lake, follow Nine Mile Canyon
Road; June-Oct. ☆ LAMONT MEADOWS. On
Nine Mile Canyon Road 13 mi. west of U.S. 395;
35 camping units; 10 trailer space accommodations;
water. ☆ LONG VALLEY. On Nine Mile Canyon
Road, 26 mi. west of U.S. 395; 18 camping units;
no trailer space; water.

McCAIN VALLEY RECREATION AREA. El. to
4,000 ft. In lower Sonoran Desert. From U.S. 80
turn north at Boulevard, 6 mi. west of Jacumba,
follow BLM road; hunting, hiking, rockhounding;
open all year. COTTONWOOD RECREATION
AREA. On McCain Valley Road, 16 mi. north of
U.S. 80; 12 camping units with trailer space; water.
LARK CANYON. On McCain Valley Road 7 mi.
north of U.S. 80; 10 camping units with 4 trailer
space accommodations; water. WHITE ARROW.
On McCain Valley Road, 15 mi. north of U.S. 80;
8 camping units with 3 trailer space accommodations;
boil water before use.

OWENS VALLEY RECREATION AREA. El. 4500
to 5000 ft. Desert valley at foot of Sierra-Nevadas;
mountains nearby to 14,495 ft. elevation; hunting,
fishing, hiking, scenery; May-Oct. ☆ GOODALE
CREEK. Off U.S. 396 to access road 1½ mi. north
of Aberdeen, north of Independence; 62 camping
units with 30 trailer space accommodations; water.
☆ HORTON CREEK. Northwest 10 mi. from
Bishop. Turn into access road from U.S. 395, follow

3 mi.; 53 camping units with 20 trailer space accommodations; water. ☆ SYMMES CREEK. Off U.S. 395, 6 mi. southwest of Independence; 55 camping units; trailer space; water.

RAMSHORN SPRINGS. El. 6000 ft. Countryside 50 mi. north of Susanville; 2.6 mi. east of U.S. 395 on Post Camp Road; hunting; 3 camping units; no trailer space; water; June-Oct.

READING ISLAND. El. 500 ft. On Sacramento River, 6 mi. east of Cottonwood, 20 mi. southeast of Redding (U.S. 99); water sports, boat launching ramp, fishing, hunting, 10 picnic sites; water; open all year. Cooperative site, BLM and Shasta County.

SUMMIT CAMP. El. 6200 ft. Mountainous country 5½ mi. east of U.S. 395 on Post Camp Road, 53 mi. north of Susanville; hunting, scenery; 4 camping units; no trailer space; boil water before use; June-Oct.

COLORADO

☆ FIVE POINT PLACER. El. 6000 ft. On Arkansas River, 17 mi. west of Canon City on U.S. 50; hiking, fishing, hunting, camping; 9 camping units with trailer space; water; year-round (14-day limit).

☆ GYPSUM. El. 6000 ft. On Eagle River, 1½ mi. west of Gypsum on U.S. 6-24; hiking, fishing, hunting, camping; 10 camping units with trailer space; water; year-round (14-day limit).

BEGGS. El. 2400 ft. Desert reservoir, 26 mi. west of Cambridge on State Highway 71; fishing, hunting, hiking, water sports, camping, scenery; 30 camping units with 15 trailer space accommodations; water ½ mi. at Brownlee Reservoir; May-Nov.

COVE. Owyhee Co. El. 3000 ft. Between Bruneau and Grandview, off State Highway 51 from 20 mi. south of Mountain Home. 26 campsites. Fishing, hunting, hiking, rockhounding. Year around.

KILLARNEY LAKE. El. 2125 ft. Mountain lake. Turn off State Highway 3, 2 mi. southwest of Rose Lake. Follow signs 4 mi. on county road, then ¼ mi. by foot trail. Boat access to lake and site from Cocur d'Alene River. Boating, fishing, hiking, water sports, swimming, picnicking, scenery; no trailer space; boil water before use; May-Sept.

MINERAL RIDGE. El. 3000 ft. Site has lake view; 9 mi. east of Coeur d'Alene on U.S. 10 to junction with U.S. 95A, southwest on U.S. 95A around east end of Coeur d'Alene Lake 2 mi. to parking area; hiking, picnicking, scenery; no trailer space; water; July-Oct.

PACK RIVER VIEWPOINT. El. 2300 ft. Lake overlook; 18 mi. east of Sandpoint on U.S. 10A; fishing, hiking, hunting, camping, scenery; 5 camping units with 3 accommodations for small trailers; water; May-Sept.

ROCHAT RECREATION COMPLEX. El. to 6000 ft. From U.S. 90 turn south at Cataldo, follow BLM

Rochat Road 32 mi. over summit to St. Joe River Highway, 9 mi. east of St. Maries. Steep mountain road (inquire locally for road conditions), trailers not recommended; fishing, hunting, hiking, scenery; June-Sept.

CRYSTAL LAKE. El. 5300 ft. Mountain lake off Alt. U.S. 95, 9 mi. east of St. Maries on Rochat Divide Road for 10 mi. then 2 mi. by trail; 2 camping units; water.

MIRROR LAKE. El. 5760 ft. Mountain lake. Interstate 90 east of Coeur d'Alene, south 9 mi. on Rochat Divide Road, east 5 mi. on Boise Peak Road, ½ mi. steep trail; 2 camping units; water.

TINGLEY SPRINGS. El. 5200 ft. Valley overlook off Alt. U.S. 95, 6 mi. east of St. Maries on St. Joe River Road, then 9 mi. north on St. Joe Baldy Lookout Road; 5 camping units; water.

☆ SALMON RIVER COMPLEX, EAST FORK. El. 5376 ft. Located at junction of East Fork and main Salmon Rivers, 18 mi. southwest of Challis on U.S. 93; mountain river, hunting, fishing, camping, scenery, hiking, rockhounding, picnicking. Historic site. 7 camping units with trailer space; May-Nov. (14-day limit).

SHEEP SPRINGS. El. 5420 ft. Mountain pass. From St. Maries east 9 mi. on the St. Joe River Road, then north on the Rochat Divide Road past the St. Joe Baldy Lookout 3 mi. to saddle between two ridges; hunting, picnicking, scenery; no trailer space; water; July-Sept.

SKOOKUMCHUCK. El. 1500 ft. Scenic river 4 mi.

south of Whitebird on U.S. 95; fishing, hiking, hunt-ing, swimming, boating, scenery; 5 camping units with space for small trailers; water; year-round.

☆ STECK. El. 2028 ft. Desert reservoir 22 mi. west of Weiser via Old Ferry Road; fishing, hunting, hiking, water sports, camping, picnicking; scenery. 23 camp-ing units with 12 trailer space accommodations; water; May-Nov.

MONTANA

MADISON RIVER RECREATION AREA. El. 5000-5900 ft. Famous stream for trout fishing, camping, hunting, scenery; near Yellowstone National Park; Apr.-Oct. ☆ RED MOUNTAIN. El. 5000 ft. Moun-tain stream 25 mi. west of Bozeman on State High-way 289 beside Madison River; 22 camping units with trailer space; water. ☆ RUBY CREEK. El. 5700 ft. Mountain stream 20 mi. south of Ennis on State Highway 287; 28 camping units with trailer space; water. ☆ SOUTH MADISON. El. 5900 ft. 25 mi. south of Ennis on State Highway 287; 18 picnic units with trailer space; water.

NEVADA

MEADOW VALLEY CAMP. El. 6000 ft. Canyon view 16 mi. east of Pioche on county road through town of Ursine; hunting, fishing, hiking, camping, scenery; 4 camping units; boil water before use; Apr.-Jan.

☆ **NORTH WILDHORSE CAMP.** El. 6270 ft. Reser-voir 77 mi. north of Elko on State Highway 43;

hiking, fishing, hunting, camping, picnicking; 15 camping units with trailer space; water; May-Nov.

☆ RED ROCK CANYON COMPLEX. — WILLOW SPRINGS. El. 4600 ft. Canyon view. West via county road 85 for 14 mi. to the Red Rocks Canyon turnoff; turn right and drive 4 mi. on BLM gravel road to springs; scenery, mountain climbing; picnicking; geologic formations; no trailer space; water; year-round.

SPORTSMAN'S BEACH. El. 4500 ft. Lake shore 15 mi. north of Hawthorne via U.S. 395; fishing, boating, water sports, hiking, picnicking, scenery, geologic formations; no trailer space; water; year-round.

TAMARACK POINT. El. 4500 ft. Lake shore, 18½ mi. north of Hawthorne on U.S. 395; west shore of Walker Lake; fishing, hiking, swimming, mountain climbing; camping; 20 camping units with trailer space; water; year-round.

NEW MEXICO

☆ ANGEL PEAK. El. 6400 ft. Badlands 13 mi. south and east of Bloomfield via State Highway 44; hiking, scenery, water sports, camping, picnicking, rock-hounding, archeological site and geologic formations; 6 camping units with trailer space; boil water before use; Mar.-Nov.

SANTA CRUZ LAKE. El. 6285 ft. Reservoir 13 mi. east of Espanola via State Highways 76 and 4; fishing, boating, hiking, swimming, camping; 25 camping units with 8 trailer space accommodations; boil water before use; Apr.-Oct.

☆ THREE RIVERS PEAROGLYPHS. El. 5100 ft.
Archeological site 33 mi. south of Carrizozo via U.S.
54; scenery, camping, hiking; 6 camping units with
trailer space; boil water before use; year-round.

ALDER GLEN. El. 250 ft. Forest stream 15 mi. northeast of Beaver via BLM Mestucca Road; fishing,
hiking, hunting, swimming, picnicking; 5 camping
units with 2 trailer space accommodations; water;
May-Oct.

ALSEA FALLS. El. 800 ft. Forest stream 6 mi. west
of Glennbrook on BLM South Fork Alsea Road;
fishing, scenery, hiking, hunting, geologic formations;
5 camping units; no trailer space; water; year-round.

☆ BEAR CREEK. El. 640 ft. Forest stream 8 mi.
southwest of Camas Valley on State Highway 42;
fishing, hiking, swimming, picnicking; 10 camping
units with trailer space; water; May-Oct.

☆ BEAVERTRAIL. El. 550 ft. Canyon stream 10.3
mi. north of Sherar's Bridge on BLM Deschutes
River Road; fishing, hunting, rockhounding, scenery;
20 camping units with 10 trailer space accommodations; water; year-round.

BLITZEN CROSSING. El. 5000 ft. Mountain stream
25 mi. south of Frenchglen on south leg of BLM
Steens Mt. loop road; fishing, hunting, scenery, camping, hiking; 5 camping units with trailer space; water
(boil before use); July-Nov.

BURNT MOUNTAIN. El. 2240 ft. Forest stream 30

mi. east of Coquille on BLM Burnt Mt. Road; scenery, hiking; 3 camping units; no trailer space, water; July-Nov.

CANYON CREEK. El. 1100 ft. Forest stream 17 mi. east of Stayton on Elkhorn County Road; fishing, swimming, scenery, picnicking; no trailer space; water; spring-summer-fall.

CAVITT CREEK FALLS. El. 1200 ft. Falls 8 mi. south of Glide on Cavitt Creek County Road; fishing, swimming, hunting, hiking, picnicking; 4 camping units with trailer space; water; May-Oct.

CHERRY CREEK-BIG TREE. El. 650 ft. Forest stream 27 mi. east of Coquille on BLM Cherry Creek Road; hiking, scenery, picnicking; no trailer space; boil water before use; May-Oct.

☆ CLAY CREEK. El. 700 ft. Forest stream 28½ mi. southeast of Mapleton via BLM Siuslaw Road; swimming, fishing, hunting, hiking; 14 camping units with 6 trailer space accommodations; water; year-round.

COLD SPRINGS. El. 3600 ft. Forested area 32 mi. west of Glendale on BLM Mt. Reuben Road; hunting, hiking, camping; 2 camping units; no trailer space; water; May-Oct.

COW LAKES. El. 4500 ft. Desert Lake 31 mi. northwest of Jordan Valley on county road; boating, fishing, hunting, camping, scenery, geologic formations; 10 camping units with trailer space; boil water before use; Apr.-Dec.

CROOKED RIVER. El. 3000 ft. Canyon stream 20 mi. south of Prineville on State Highway 27 about 3 mi. downstream from Prineville Reservoir; fishing, hunting, scenery, rockhounding, picnicking; no trailer space; water; year-round.

DARBY CREEK. El. 1000 ft. Creek 20 mi. southwest of Riddle on BLM Cow Creek Road; scenery, picnicking; boil water before use; Apr.-Oct.

DEER CREEK. El. 1480 ft. Stream located 6 mi. east of Selma on Deer Creek County Road; camping, hunting; 30 camping units with 14 trailer space accommodations; water; Apr.-Oct.

DOGWOOD. El. 1150 ft. Forest stream 19 mi. northeast of Foster on BLM Quartzville Road; fishing, hiking, scenery, picnicking; no trailer space; water; spring-summer-fall.

ELDERBERRY FLAT. El. 2000 ft. Stream 30 mi. north of Gold Hill on BLM West Fork Evans Creek access road; camping, hunting, scenery, picnicking; 12 camping units with 10 trailer space accommodations; boil water before use; Mar.-Nov.

☆ ELKHORN VALLEY. El. 975 ft. Canyon view 20 mi. east of Stayton on Elkhorn County Road; fishing, swimming, scenery, hiking, camping, hunting, picnicking; 12 camping units with 3 trailer space accommodations; water; May-Oct. (May be used year-round).

☆ FISHERMEN'S BEND. El. 800 ft. on river, 1½ mi. west of Mill City on State Highway 22; fishing, swimming, scenery, hiking, camping, picnicking; 40 camping units with 20 trailer space accommodations; water; May-Oct. (9-day limit.)

☆ GERBER RESERVOIR. El. 4800 ft. Reservoir in

pine forest 18 mi. south of Bly; fishing, boating, hunting, camping; 50 camping units with trailer space; 2 boat ramps; water; May-Oct.

GOLD NUGGET. El. 1100 ft. On river 2 mi. north of Gold Hill on State Highway 234; fishing, scenery, picnicking; no trailer space; water, except in winter; year-round.

GUNTER. El. 1000 ft. On river 15 mi. northwest of Drain on Smith River County Road; fishing, hiking, hunting, camping, picnicking; 5 camping units with 4 trailer space accommodations; water; May-Oct.

HAIGHT CREEK. El. 600 ft. Forest stream 28 mi. west of Eugene on BLM Siuslaw Road; scenery, fishing, picnicking; no trailer space; water; year-round.

JACKMAN PARK. El. 8000 ft. In aspen thicket 17 mi. east of Frenchglen on BLM Steens Mt. Road; fishing, hunting, scenery, camping, hiking, geologic formations; 4 camping units with trailer space; water; July-Oct.

LAKE CREEK. El. 500 ft. Forest stream 35 mi. west of Junction City off State Highway 36; fishing, hiking, picnicking; no trailer space; water; summer.

LITTLE APPLEGATE. El. 2500 ft. On stream 19 mi. southeast of Applegate on BLM road; fishing, hiking, hunting, picnicking; no trailer space; water; Mar-Nov.

LITTLE BEND. El. 600 ft. Forest stream 8 mi. north of Mountaindale on East Fork Dairy Creek County Road; fishing, scenery, hiking, picnicking; no trailer space; water; year-round.

LONE ROCK. El. 800 ft. On river 2 mi. east of Glide

on Lone Rock County Road; fishing, picnicking; no trailer space; water; July-Sept.

☆ LOON LAKE. El. 1500 ft. Mountain lake 20 mi. southeast of Reedsport on Loon Lake County Road; swimming, fishing, boating, hunting, picnicking; 75 camping units with trailer space; water; May-Oct.

MIDDLE CREEK. El. 400 ft. Forest stream 6 mi. northeast of McKinley on BLM Middle Creek access road; fishing, hiking, 1 camping unit; no trailer space; boil water before use; May-Nov.

MILL CREEK. El. 550 ft. Forest stream 2½ mi. south of Buell on Mill Creek County Road; fishing, scenery, hiking, hunting, swimming, picnicking, geologic formations; no trailer space; water; year-round.

☆ MILL POND. El. 1120 ft. Creek 4 mi. northeast of Idleyld Park on BLM Rock Creek Road; swimming, fishing, hiking, camping, hunting, picnicking; 11 camping units with 4 trailer space accommodations; large shelter with electricity and stoves; water; May-Oct.

MISSOURI BEND. El. 250 ft. Forest stream 12 mi. west of Alsea on State Highway 34; fishing, boating, scenery, hunting, swimming, hiking, picnicking, geologic formations; no trailer space; water; year-round.

NORTH FORK EAGLE CREEK. El. 600 ft. Mountain stream 8 mi. northeast of Estacada on North Fork Eagle Creek County Road; fishing, hunting, hiking, camping; 15 camping units with 5 trailer space accommodations; water; May-Oct.

☆ PAGE SPRING. El. 4250 ft. Mountain stream 62

mi. southeast of Burns on Donner and Blitzen River; fishing, hunting, scenery, camping; 25 camping units with 20 trailer space accommodations; water; June-Sept.

PALMER BUTTE. El. 2000 ft. Mountain top 8 mi. east of Brookings on Gardiner Ridge Road; scenery, picnicking; no trailer space; boil water before use; Apr.-Nov.

☆ PARK CREEK. El. 400 ft. Forest stream 26 mi. east of Coquille on BLM Middle Creek Road; swimming, hunting, hiking; 12 camping units with trailer space; water; May-Oct.

☆ ROCK CREEK. El. 1280 ft. Creek 5 mi. northeast of Idleyld on BLM Rock Creek Road; fishing, swimming, hiking, hunting, camping, picnicking; 16 camping units with 7 trailer space accommodations; water; May-Oct.

ROGUE RIVER TRAIL. El. 500-800 ft. Hiking trail along famous white water stream beginning 29 mi. northwest of Grants Pass at junction of Graves Creek and Rogue River; hiking, fishing, scenery. Trail ends at Tucker Flat, accessible by car; water available along trail but should be boiled before use. Mar.-Nov. BIG SLIDE. 3.7 mi. downriver on Rogue River Trail; 3 camping units; no trailer space. KELSEY CREEK. 15.4 mi. downriver on Rogue River Trail; 3 camping units; no trailer space. RAINIE FALLS. 1.7 mi. downriver on Rogue River Trail; 2 camping units; no trailer space. RUSSIAN CREEK. 5.7 mi. downriver on Rogue River Trail; 1 camping unit; no trailer space. TUCKER FLAT. 23.4 mi. downriver on Rogue River Trail, 53 miles northwest of Grants Pass via Grave Creek and Kelsey Roads; 8 camping units with 5 trailer space accommodations.

SCAPONIA. El. 600 ft. Forest stream 7 mi. northeast of Veronia on Veronia-Scappoose County Road; fishing, hiking, hunting, scenery, picnicking; 4 camping units with 3 trailer space accommodations; water; May-Oct. (May be used yearlong).

☆ SCAREDMAN CREEK. El. 1440 ft. Creek 5 mi. north of Steamboat on BLM Canton Creek Road; hiking, hunting, swimming, picnicking; 10 camping units with 5 trailer space accommodations; water; May-Oct.

SHADY BRANCH. El. 3150 ft. Forested area 25 mi. northwest of Grants Pass on BLM Galice and Silver Creek Roads; hunting, hiking, camping; 2 camping units; no trailer space; water; May-Oct.

☆ SHARP'S CREEK. El. 1200 ft. Forest stream 25 mi. southeast of Cottage Grove via Sharp's Creek County Road; swimming, fishing, hiking; 10 camping units with 8 trailer space accommodations; water; year-round.

☆ SIXES RIVER. El. 160 ft. Forest stream 11 mi. east of Sixes on Sixes River County Road; fishing, swimming, hunting, hiking; 19 camping units with trailer space; water; June-Sept. (14 day limit unless specified.)

SMITH RIVER FALLS. El. 150 ft. Forest stream 30 mi. east of Gardiner on BLM Smith River Road; swimming, fishing, hunting; 6 camping units; no trailer space; boil water before use; May-Oct.

SOUTH JETTY ROAD. On ocean 2 mi. south of Florence on U.S. 101. Scenery, fishing, hiking, picnicking; no trailer space; boil water before use; year-round.

SURVEYOR. El. 5200 ft. Forested area 33 mi. east of Ashland via BLM Keno Road; hiking, hunting, camping; 6 camping units with 4 trailer space accommodations; water; June-Oct.

SUSAN CREEK FALLS. El. 2000 ft. Falls 29 mi. east of Roseburg on State Highway 138; scenery, hiking, picnicking, historic site; no trailer space; boil water before use; July-Sept.

☆ TOPSY. El. 3800 ft. Reservoir 8 mi. west of Keno on Topsy County Road; swimming, boating, fishing, hiking, hunting, camping; 6 camping units with 4 trailer space accommodations; water; Mar.-Dec.

TUNNEL RIDGE. El 2250 ft. Fishing stream 16 mi. southeast of Applegate on BLM Road; hiking, hunting, picnicking; no trailer space; boil water before use; Mar.-Nov.

TURNER CREEK. El. 250 ft. Forest stream 6.7 mi. east of Mapleton on State Highway 126; fishing, hunting, hiking; 8 camping units with trailer space; water; year-round.

☆ TYEE. El. 320 ft. On river 15 mi. northwest of Sutherlin on Umpqua River; fishing, swimming, camping, hiking, hunting, picnicking; 11 camping units with 4 trailer space accommodations; small shelter available; water; May-Oct.

VINCENT CREEK. El. 200 ft. Forest stream 35 mi. east of Gardiner on BLM Smith River Road; fishing, hiking; 12 camping units; no trailer space; water; Apr.-Nov.

☆ WHITTAKER CREEK. El. 300 ft. Forest stream 14 mi. southeast of Mapleton on BLM Whittaker Creek Road; fishing, swimming, picnicking, hiking, hunting; 11 camping units with 7 trailer space accommodations; water; year-round.

WOLF CREEK FALLS. El. 1200 ft. Falls 10 mi. southeast of Glide on Little River County Road; scenery, hiking, picnicking; no trailer space; boil water before use; July-Sept.

☆ YELLOWBOTTOM. El. 1600 ft. Mountain stream 23 mi. northeast of Foster on BLM Quartzville Road; fishing, scenery, hiking, camping, hunting, swimming; 19 camping units with 5 trailer space accommodations; water; May-Oct. (May be used yearlong).

UTAH

☆ CALF CREEK. El. 5500 ft. Canyon stream 15 mi. northeast of Escalante, adjacent to State Highway 54; hiking, scenery; 9 camping units with trailer space; boil water before use; Mar.-Oct.

☆ CANYON RIMS RECREATION AREA. El. 6000 ft. Overlooks Canyonlands area. On BLM road off U.S. 160 turn west 22 mi. north of Monticello; historic site, geologic formations; hiking, scenery. Apr-Oct. ☆ ANTICLINE OVERLOOK. Plateau, canyon views, picnicking; no trailer space; boil water before use. ☆ HATCH POINT CAMPGROUND. Plateau, canyon views; 10 camping units with trailer space; water; 23 mi. from U.S. 160. ☆ NEEDLES OVERLOOK. Plateau, canyon views; picnicking; no trailer space; boil water before use. ☆ WINDWHISTLE

CAMPGROUND. Plateau 5½ mi. from U.S. 160; 20 camping units with 13 trailer space accommodations; water.

CEDAR MT. OVERLOOK. El. 7600 ft. Plateau 24 mi. via county road, southeast of Cleveland on State Highway 155; scenery, hiking, picnicking, historic site, geologic formations; no trailer space; boil water before use. Apr.-Oct.

HOG SPRINGS. El. 4000 ft. Walled canyon 36 mi. southeast of Hanksville via State Highway 95. Archeological site, picnicking; no trailer space; water; year-round.

LONESOME BEAVER CAMPGROUND. El. 7500 ft. In mountains 23 mi. south of Hanksville off State Highway 24; hiking, hunting, camping, historic site. Primitive road, not recommended for passenger cars hauling trailers; 4 camping units; water; June-Oct.

McMILLAN SPRING CAMPGROUND. El. 9500 ft. In mountains 25 mi. south of Hanksville via State Highway 95 then 2½ mi. west of Trachite Junction via dirt road. Hiking, hunting, camping, historic site. Primitive road, not recommended for passenger cars hauling trailers; 10 camping units; water; June-Oct.

☆ PRICE CANYON. El. 7500 ft. Mountain canyon 15 mi. north of Price, 2½ mi. southwest off U.S. 50-6; hiking, hunting, camping, scenery; 19 camping units with 2 trailer space accommodations; water; May-Oct.

☆ RED CLIFFS. El. 3500 ft. Desert canyon 4½ mi. southwest of Leeds off U.S. 91 via Frontage Road and BLM road; hiking, hunting, camping; 10 camping units with 10 trailer space accommodations; water; year-round.

SAN RAFAEL CAMPGROUND. El. 5500 ft. In desert 20 mi. southeast of Castle Dale off State Highway 10 on San Rafael Road; archeological site, Indian writing, hiking, camping; 10 camping units with trailer space; water; Apr.-Oct.

WYOMING

FOURTEEN MILE. El. 6800 ft. Roadside rest and fishing pond 14 mi. north of Rock Springs on U.S. 187. Camping, overnight picnicking; no trailer space; water; year-round.

☆ FIVE SPRINGS FALLS CAMPGROUND. El. 6800 ft. Falls and mountain stream 23 mi. east of Lovell on State Highway 14; scenery, hiking, hunting, camping, overnight picnicking, rockhounding, mountain climbing; geologic formations; 4 camping units with trailer space; water; June-Oct.

☆ GREEN MT.-COTTONWOOD CAMPGROUND. El. 8500 ft. Mountain stream setting located on improved road 8 mi. south of U.S. 287. Enter road 6 mi. east of Jeffrey City. Fishing, hunting, camping, picnicking, scenery, hiking, rockhounding; 19 camping units with 5 trailer space accommodations; water; June-Oct.

☆ GREEN MT. WILD HORSE POINT OVERLOOK & PICNIC GROUND. El. 9060 ft. Pleasant overlook located on improved road 11 mi. south of U.S. 287. Enter road 6 mi. east of Jeffrey City. Fishing, hunting, picnicking, scenery, hiking, rockhounding, geologic formations; no trailer space; boil water before use; June-Oct.

BUREAU OF LAND MANAGEMENT
LAND OFICES

Alaska:
555 Cordova St.
Anchorage, Alaska   99501

516 Second Ave.
Fairbanks, Alaska   99701

Arizona:
Federal Bldg., Room 204
Phoenix, Ariz.   85025

California:
Federal Bldg., Room 4017
Sacramento, Calif.   95814
1414 Eighth St.
Riverside, Calif.   92502

Colorado:
14027 Federal Bldg.
Denver, Colo.   80202

Idaho:
323 Federal Bldg.
Boise, Idaho   83701

Montana:
(N. Dak., S. Dak.):
Federal Bldg.
316 North 26th St.
Billings, Mont.   59101

Nevada:
Federal Bldg., 300 Booth St.
Reno, Nev.   89505

New Mexico (Okla):
Federal Bldg.
Santa Fe, N. Mex.   87501

Oregon:
729 Northeast Oregon St.
Portland, Oreg.   97232

Utah:
Eighth Floor, Federal Bldg.
125 South State St.
P.O. Box 11505
Salt Lake City, Utah   84110

Washington:
729 Northeast Oregon St.
Portland, Oreg.   97232

Wyoming (Nebr., Kan.):
2120 Capitol Ave.
Cheyenne, Wyo.   82001

All Other States:
Robin Bldg.
7981 Eastern Ave.
Silver Spring, Md.   20910

Dealers and Outfitters
Listed Alphabetically by State

SYMBOLS: (A) Mountaineering and backpack equipment; (B) General camping and outdoor equipment; (C) Other specialties; * Catalog available.

ALASKA

Buness Brothers (B)
Wrangell, 99929

Hammer & Wikan (B)
Box 249
Petersburg, 99833

Rusher's Juneau Young Co. (B)
Juneau, 99801

Skinner's (B)
118 Seward
Juneau, 99801

ARIZONA

Cap Trails (C)
(Packs, tents)
3920 West Clarendon
Phoenix, 85019

CALIFORNIA

Abercrombie & Fitch (B)*
220 Post St.
San Francisco, 94108

Ames-Harris-Neville (B)
2800 17th St.
San Francisco, 94110

Antelope Camping Equipment (B)
10268 Imperial Ave.
Cupertino, 95514

Cutter Laboratories (Snakebite & Insect Kits
4th & Parker St.,
Berkeley, 94710

Gerry Mountain Sports (B)*
228 Grant St.
San Francisco, 95014

Highland Outfitters (B)*
3579 University Ave.
P. O. Box 121
Riverside, 92502

Himalayan Industries (C)*
(Pack frames, bags)
807 Cannery Row
P. O. Box 950
Monterey, 93940

Kelty Pack, Inc. (C)*
Mountaineer Packs
Victory Blvd.
P. O. Box 3453
Glendale, 91201

Sierra Mountain Equipment (A)*
2211 California St.
P. O. Box 15251
San Francisco, 94115

Sports Chalet (A)*
951 Foothill Blvd.
P. O. Box 626
La Canada, 91011

The North Face (A)*
Alpine Equipment Specialists
308 Columbus Ave.
San Francisco, 94133

The North Face (A)*
700 Welch Rd.
Palo Alto,   94300

5 Country Club Plaza
Orinda,   94563

2804 Telegraph Ave.
Berkeley,   94705

The Ski Hut (Trailwise) (A)*
1615 University Ave.
Berkeley,   94703

Sierra Designs (C)*
4th & Addison Sts.
Berkeley,   94710

Swiss Ski Sports (B)
559 Clay St.
San Francisco,   94111

COLORADO

Alp Sport (C)
3245 Prairie Ave.
P. O. Box 1081
Boulder,   80302

Colorado Outdoors Sports (A)*
Gerry Division
5450 N. Valley Highway
Denver,   80216

Dave Cooks Sporting Goods (B)*
1603A Larimer St.
Denver,   80202

Gart Brothers (B)*
Sporting Goods Company
1643 Larimer St.
Denver,   80202

Holubar Mountaineering (A)*
Retail stores in Boulder, Denver
P. O. Box 7
Boulder, 80302

Sportsman Products (C)
Plastic snowshoes
P. O. Box 1082
Boulder,   80302

Survival Research Laboratories (A)*
Air-Land-Sea-Trail Survival Kits
17 Marland Rd.
Colorado Springs,   80906

Frostline Outdoor Equipment (C)*
Do-it-yourself kits
P. O. Box 1378
Boulder,   80302

ILLINOIS

Kien's Sporting Goods (B)*
227 W. Washington
Chicago,   60606

MAINE

L. L. Bean (B)*
278 Maine St.
Freeport,   04032

MARYLAND

Bishop's Outdoor Equipment (C)
6804 Millwood Rd.
Bethesda,   20034

H & H Surplus Center (B)*
Catalog 25 cents.
1028 West Baltimore
Baltimore,   21223

MASSACHUSETTS

Corcoran, Inc. (B)*
Stoughton,   02072

Don Gleason's Camper's Supply (B)
Catalog 25 cents.
9 Pearl St.
Northampton,   01060

Moor & Mountain (B)
14 Main St.
Concord,   01742
Eastern Mountain Sports, Inc. (B)
1041 Commonwealth Ave.
Boston,   02215
Wellesley,   02181
Springfield,   01101

MINNESOTA

Gokey Company (B)*
21 West Fifth St.
St. Paul,   55102
Herter's Inc. (B)*
Catalog 50 cents.
Rural Route 1
Waseca,   56093

MISSOURI

Gateway Sporting Goods (B)*
3177 Mercier Street
Kansas City,   64111

NEW HAMPSHIRE

Peter Limmer & Sons (B)
Intervale,   03845

NEW JERSEY

Morsan — Outfitters (B)*
810 Route 17
Paramus,   07652
Farmingdale, N. Y.,   11375

NEW YORK

Abercrombie & Fitch (B)*
Madison Ave. at 45th St.
New York,   10017

Thomas Black & Sons (B)*
Catalog 25 cents.
930 Ford St.
Ogdensburg,   13669
Camp & Trail Outfitters (A)*
Catalog 25 cents.
112 Chambers St.
New York,   10007
Gloy's (B)
11 Addison St.
Larchmont,   10538
Walter E. Stern (B)
254 Nagle Ave.
New York,   10034
Parker Distributors (B)
40 Industrial Place
New Rochelle,   10805
Mountaineering Supply (B)
897 St. David's Lane
Schenectady,   12309

OKLAHOMA

P & S Sales (B)*
P. O. Box 155
Tulsa,   74102

OREGON

Alaska Sleeping Bag Co. (A)*
701 N. W. Dawson Way
Beaverton,   97005
Alpine Hut (A)*
1250 Loyd Center
Portland,   97232
Norm Thomson (B)*
Outfitters
1805 N. W. Thurman
Portland,   97209

PENNSYLVANIA

I. Goldberg (B)*
429 Market St.
Philadelphia, 19106
Survival Equip. Co. (C)*
Berkes County,
Oley, 19547

TEXAS

B & S Outfitters (B)*
P. O. Box 8
Hooks, 75561

WASHINGTON

Alpine Hut, Inc. (A)*
2650 University Village
Seattle, 98105
Alpine Hut (A)*
420 Tacoma Mall
Tacoma, 98409
Alpine Hut (A)*
Renton Shopping Center
Renton, 98055
Alpine Hut, Inc. (A)*
Central Offices
Mail Order Division
4725 30th Ave. N. E.
Seattle, 98105
Eddie Bauer (A)*
Outfitter
417 East Pine St.
Seattle, 98122
Recreational Equipment Inc. (A)*
1525 11th Ave.
Seattle, 98122

WISCONSIN

Gander Mountain, Inc. (B)*
Outfitters
P. O. Box 248
Wilmot, 53192
Laacke & Joys Co. (B)*
1433 North Water St.
Milwaukee, 53202

DISTRICT OF COLUMBIA

The Trading Post (B)
3336 N. St.
Washington, D. C., 20004

CANADA

The T Eaton Company (B)
190 Yonge St.
Toronto, 1
Simpson-Sears Ltd. (B)
108 Mutual St.
Toronto, 2
Premier Cycle & Sports (B)
Mountaineering outfitters
319 Seventh Ave., S. W.
Calgary
Arlberg Sports Haus (B)
Outfitters
816 W. Pender St.
Vancouver, 1
Woodwards (B)
Hastings & Abbot St.
Vancouver, 3
Thomas Black & Sons (A)*
Catalog 25 cents.
225 Strathcona Ave.
Ottawa, 3

Sources of Emergency Rations & Dehydrated Foods

Ann Benedict's
Dri-Lite Foods
11333 Atlantic Ave.
Lynwood, Calif.   90262

Ad Seidel Trail Packets
1245 W. Dickens Ave.
Chicago, Ill.   60014

Bernard's Food Industries
(East of Rocky Mountains)
217 N. Jefferson St.
Chicago, Ill.   60606
(West of Rocky Mountains)
222 South 24th St.
P.O. Box 487
San Jose, Calif.   95103
(Canada)
120 Sunrise Ave.
Toronto, Ontario Canada

Chuck Wagon
Survival Food Packs
P.O. Box 66
Newton, Mass.   01355

Cramore Fruit Products
90 West Broadawy
New York, N.Y.   10007

E-Z Food Products Company
1420 So. Western Ave.
Gardena, Calif.   90247

Firefly Survival Rations
Coast Guard Type
Safety Research & Mfg. Co.
Seattle, Wash.   90104

H & M Packing Corporation
(Survival Packs 3-8-14 day kits)
915 Ruberta Ave.
Glendale, Calif.   91201

Lyon's Food Specials
P.O. Box 11215
Los Angeles, Calif.   90011

Mergen Industries
6808 Marshall Rd.
Upper Darby, Pa.   19082

Seidel Trail Packets
David Abercrombie Company
97 Chambers St.
New York, N.Y.   10007

Stow-A-Way Products
Survival Foods
Freeze-Dri & Dehydrated Foods
Cohasset, Mass.   02025

Trail Meals
J. B. Kisky
1829 N.E. Alberta St.
Portland, Ore.   97211

Trailwise Ski Hut
1615 University Ave.
Berkeley, Calif.   94702

Trip-Lites
S. Gumpett
812 Jersey Ave.
Jersey City, N. J.   07302

Tripperoos
Hilker & Bletsch
614 Hubbard St.
Chicago, Ill.   60609

Trail Feeding Specialties
Box 441
Summit, N. J.   07901

Survival Research Laboratories
17 Marland Rd.
Colorado Springs, Colo.   80906

BOOKS

The following books may be obtained from your local bookstore, mountain equipment outfitter, or city or county library.

American National Red Cross. *First Aid Textbook*. New York: Doubleday, 1970.

Angier, Bradford. *Free for the Eating*. Harrisburg, Pa.: Stackpole Books, 1966. You can live off the country under emergency conditions and survive.

————. *Home in Your Pack*. Harrisburg, Pa.; Stackpole Books, 1965. Details on where to go and what to take.

————. *Skills for Taming the Wilds*. Harrisburg, Pa.: Stackpole Books, 1967.

————. *Wilderness Cookery*. Harrisburg, Pa.: Stackpole Books, 1960. Nothing more important to an outdoorsman, hiker, or backpacker than grub!

Back, Joe. *Horses, Hitches, and Rocky Trails*. Chicago: The Swallow Press.

Bates, Joseph D. *The Outdoor Cook's Bible*. New York: Doubleday, 1964. Authority for outdoor cooking.

Brower, David R., Ed. *Going Light with Backpack or Burro*. San Francisco: Sierra Club Book, 1956.

————. *The Sierra Club Wilderness Handbook*. San Francisco: Sierra Club Book.

————. *Ski Mountaineering*, Rev. Ed. San Francisco: Sierra Club Book, 1962.

Caldwell, John R. *The Cross-Country Ski Book*, Rev. Ed. Brattleboro, Vt.: Stephen Greene Press, 1968.

Crew, Peter. *Dictionary of Mountaineering.* Harrisburg, Pa.: Stackpole Books, 1969. Reference on mountain features, climbing technique and equipment.

Fletcher, Colin. *The Thousand Miles Summer.* Howell North. 1964.

———. *Walking Through Time.* Knopf. 1968.

———. *The Complete Walker.* Knopf. 1968.

Henderson, Kenneth A. *Handbook of American Mountaineering.* Boston: Houghton Mifflin Company.

Kjellstrom, Bjorn. *Be Expert with Map and Compass.* Harrisburg, Pa.: Stackpole Books, 1968. An entertaining short course in using maps and compass.

Macfarlan, Allan A. *Boy's Book of Hiking.* Harrisburg, Pa.: Stackpole Books, 1968. Suggestions for more than 50 city, suburban, and country hikes; tells about overnight hikes, gear, safety.

Mendenhall, Ruth and John. *Introduction to Rock and Mountain Climbing.* Harrisburg, Pa.: Stackpole Books, 1969.

Merrill, W. K. *All About Camping.* Harrisburg, Pa.: Stackpole Books, 1963. Hiking, camping, backpacking, survival.

———. *Getting Out of Outdoor Trouble.* Harrisburg, Pa.: Stackpole Books, 1965. A civilian survival book.

———. *The Hunter's Bible.* New York: Doubleday, 1968. Where to go, what to take, and how to hunt in back country. Large section on first aid and survival.

Miracle, Leonard and Decker, Maurice H. *Complete Book on Camping.* New York: Harper & Row, 1962.

Ormond, Clyde. *Complete Book of Outdoor Lore.* New York: Harper & Row, 1965.

Osgood, William E. and Hurley, Leslie J. *Ski Touring.* Rutland, Vt.: Charles E. Tuttle Co., Inc., 1969.

Riviere, Bill. *The Camper's Bible,* Rev. Ed. New York: Doubleday, 1970. Camp the way the experts do.

Starr, Walter A., Jr. *Guide to the John Muir Trail.* San Francisco: Sierra Club Books.

Sutton, Ann and Myron. *The Appalachian Trail.* New York: J. B. Lippincott Co., 1967.

Whelen, Townsend and Angier, Bradford. *On Your Own in the Wilderness.* Harrisburg, Pa.: Stackpole Books, 1958.

PAMPHLETS, BROCHURES

Cutter, Robert, M.D. *Light Weight Outing Equipment Check List;* Write to Sierra Club Foundation, 1050 Mills Tower, San Francisco, 94104 (Price is 25 cents).

Outdoors Foundation Commission. *The PTC Relays.* Pacific Crest Trail, Warren L. Rogers, President, 2729 So. Popular St., Santa Ana, California 92704.

It's a good idea to write for the Potomac-Appalachian Trail Club's catalog, *Lightweight Equipment for Hiking, Camping, and Mountaineering,* priced at its last printing at a dollar. It is currently being updated and should be available soon. From PATC, 1718 N. Street N.W., Washington, D.C. 20036.

For complete list of books on the Appalachian Trail System, write the Appalachian Trail Conference, 1718 N St., N.W., Washington, D. C. 20036, for their Publication No. 17; also to The Appalachian Mountain Club, 5 Joy St., Boston, Mass. 02108, for a list of their publications. For Pacific Crest Trail, write Information and Education, U.S. Forest Service, 630 Sansome St., San Francisco, 94111, or the Forest Service Pacific Northwest Regional Office, P.O. Box 3623, Portland, Oregon 97212.

ACKNOWLEDGMENTS

The production of this handbook on hiking and backpacking would have been almost impossible without the kind assistance and suggestions of many outdoor specialists and organizations. The author wishes to acknowledge his deep appreciation to the following: The Hon. Orville L. Freeman; The Hon. Steward L. Udall; George B. Hartzog, Jr., Director, National Park Service, Department of the Interior; Edward P. Cliff, Chief, United States Forest Service; The Chiefs of Information and Photographic Divisions of the Park and Forest Services; Fred J. Overly, Regional Director, Northwest Region, U. S. Bureau of Outdoor Recreation; The Bureau of Land Management, United States Department of the Interior; Col. Frank R. Wilkinson, former Commandant, United States Marine Corps Cold Weather Training Center; The California Department of Fish and Game; The Boy Scouts of America; Forest Supervisor H. D. Chriswell, Mount Baker National Forest; The Wilderness Society; The Canadian Government Travel Bureau; The various American and Canadian hiking and mountain climbing clubs; The American National Red Cross; Robert K. Cutter, M.D. of Cutter Laboratories; Roy W. Walholm, Jr., Executive Director, Survival Research Laboratories; Duncan Dwelle of The North Face Alpine Outfitters; The Alpine Hut Outfitters; The Colorado Outdoors Sports Corporation; The Alaska Sleeping Bag Company, Mountaineer Equipment; The Sierra Club of California; The Appalachian Trail Conference and the Appalachian Mountain Club.

To each of these and to the many who have helped, but are not named here, again my sincere appreciation.